Black Briar Advisors

The Marketing Edition
Master's of Influence

Lessons from America's Greatest Sales, Marketing, and Advertising Minds

Stephen L. Nalley DBA., CHA
American Business Magnate, Entrepreneur, Veteran and Author

Black Briar Advisors

Copyright © 2024
All Rights Reserved
ISBN: 9798332697630

Acknowledgment

I would like to acknowledge everyone who has ever wronged me, betrayed me, doubted me, gave up on me and/or ever tried to cheat me. You are my compelling "WHY" that has driven me to such heights. Your hate, negativity and disrespect has always motivated me to barrel through any setback and every adversity I have ever faced in my life.

I would never have set the bar so high and gone so far if it were not for you and your actions. You know who you are, and I would like to thank you all for providing me with the inspiration that I needed to drive my passion and achieve my own definition of success in my life.

About the Author

Stephen Nalley is an American Business Magnate, Entrepreneur, Investor, Veteran and Author. He is best known as the principal founder of Inner Circle Capital, Breanna Bailey Investments and Black Briar Advisors.

Over the course of Nalley's 30-year professional career, he has started and/or participated in hundreds of corporate ventures and managed over $2 Billion in Real Estate Assets.

Prior to his professional pursuits, Nalley served his country honorably in the United States Army as a Non-Commission Officer and Commando with the Army's Elite 10th Mountain Division.

After serving his Country, Nalley went on to obtain academic degrees from several prestigious colleges. Nalley earned a Bachelor of Science Degree in Healthcare Administration from the University of North Florida, Master's Degree in Business Administration and Doctorate Degree in Business Administration from the University of Atlanta and a Law Degree from the Washington University School of Law.

Stephen is a Certified Hotel Administrator through the American Hotel & Lodging Association and is a Member of the Forbes Business Council, as well as, a Writer for the Entrepreneur Leadership Network

Preface

Marketing has always been a powerful tool for shaping human behavior, driving sales, and building brands. Throughout history, there have been influential figures who have not only mastered the art of marketing but also revolutionized it. They have left an indelible mark on the industry, shaping the way we understand and practice marketing today. This book, Masters of Influence - Lessons from America's Greatest Sales, Marketing, and Advertising Minds, is a tribute to these pioneers and a guide for anyone looking to harness the power of influence in marketing.

Overview of the Book's Purpose

The primary purpose of this book is to delve into the minds of America's most iconic figures in sales, marketing, and advertising, uncovering the principles and strategies that made them successful. Each chapter provides an in-depth look at one of these masters, exploring their biographies, contributions, and the timeless lessons they have left behind. By understanding their journeys and methodologies, readers can gain valuable insights and practical knowledge to apply in their own marketing endeavors. Importance of Learning from the Masters

Learning from the masters is crucial for several reasons. Firstly, these individuals have set the standards for excellence in marketing. Their innovative approaches and groundbreaking campaigns have not only achieved remarkable results but have also transformed the industry. By studying their work, we can learn the core principles and strategies that drive successful marketing.

Secondly, the challenges they faced and overcame are often similar to those we encounter today. Understanding how they navigated these challenges can provide us with strategies and frameworks to tackle our own marketing problems. Moreover, their stories serve as a source of inspiration, showing us that creativity, persistence, and a deep understanding of human behavior are key ingredients for success.
Brief Introduction of the Key Figures to Be Discussed

This book covers a diverse group of marketing legends, each of whom has contributed uniquely to the field:

- David Ogilvy: Often referred to as the Father of Advertising, Ogilvy's emphasis on research, big ideas, and creative discipline set new standards in the industry.

- Philip Kotler: Known as the Father of Modern Marketing, Kotler's theories on consumer behavior, market segmentation, and the 4 Ps have shaped marketing as an academic discipline and practical field.

- Mary Kay Ash: Founder of Mary Kay Cosmetics, Ash's innovative direct sales model and focus on empowering women transformed the beauty industry.

- Seth Godin: A modern marketing guru, Godin's

concepts of permission marketing, tribes, and authenticity have redefined how brands connect with audiences.

- Steve Jobs: Co-founder of Apple, Jobs' visionary approach to product design, user experience, and branding revolutionized multiple industries.

- Gary Vaynerchuk: A pioneer in social media and digital marketing, Vaynerchuk's strategies for content creation, personal branding, and community engagement have set new benchmarks.

- Dan Kennedy: A master of direct response marketing, Kennedy's principles of crafting compelling offers and measuring ROI remain relevant today.

- Rosser Reeves: Known for developing the Unique Selling Proposition (USP), Reeves' work emphasized the importance of clear, distinctive messaging.

- Claude Hopkins: A pioneer of scientific advertising, Hopkins' data-driven approach and emphasis on testing and optimization laid the groundwork for modern marketing analytics.

Outline of What Readers Can Expect to Learn

Each chapter of this book is structured to provide a comprehensive understanding of the featured marketing master and their contributions. Here is a brief overview of what readers can expect:

Chapter 2: David Ogilvy - The Father of Advertising

- Biography and career highlights
- Core principles and philosophies
- Key campaigns and their impact
- Lessons on copywriting and brand image
- Modern applications of Ogilvy's methods

Chapter 3: Philip Kotler - The Father of Modern Marketing

- Biography and contributions to marketing theory
- Evolution of marketing from Kotler's perspective
- Understanding consumer behavior and market segmentation
- The 4 Ps of Marketing (Product, Price, Place, Promotion)
- Applying Kotler's principles in the digital age

Chapter 4: Mary Kay Ash - Empowerment and Direct Sales

- Biography and the founding of Mary Kay Cosmetics
- The philosophy of empowering women through sales
- The importance of personal connections in marketing

- Strategies for building a loyal salesforce and customer base
- Legacy and lasting impact on direct sales marketing

Chapter 5: Seth Godin - The Modern Marketing Guru

- Biography and key contributions to marketing
- Understanding permission marketing
- The concept of tribes and community building
- The importance of authenticity and storytelling
- Case studies of successful campaigns inspired by Godin's ideas

Chapter 6: Steve Jobs - The Art of Innovation and Branding

- Biography and impact on the technology industry
- Jobs' approach to product design and user experience
- The role of storytelling in Apple's marketing
- Key lessons from Apple's most iconic campaigns
- The importance of vision and leadership in branding

Chapter 7: Gary Vaynerchuk - Social Media and Digital Marketing

- Biography and rise to prominence
- The power of social media in modern marketing
- Content creation and personal branding

strategies
- Engaging with audiences and building a community
- Tips for leveraging digital platforms to grow a brand

Chapter 8: Dan Kennedy - Direct Response Marketing

- Biography and career achievements
- The fundamentals of direct response marketing
- Techniques for crafting compelling offers
- Case studies of successful direct response campaigns
- Integrating direct response principles into broader marketing strategies

Chapter 9: Rosser Reeves - The Unique Selling Proposition

- Biography and key contributions to advertising
- Understanding the Unique Selling Proposition (USP)
- Creating and communicating a strong USP
- Case studies of campaigns featuring effective USPs
- Applying USP concepts to modern marketing challenges

Chapter 10: Claude Hopkins - Scientific Advertising

- Biography and career highlights
- The principles of scientific advertising
- The importance of testing and measuring

results
- Techniques for writing effective copy
- Lessons from Hopkins' campaigns that remain relevant today

Chapter 11: Shaping the Future - Integrating Lessons from the Masters

- Synthesis of key lessons from each master
- Strategies for integrating these lessons into modern marketing
- Adapting to future marketing trends and challenges
- Building a legacy of influence and success in marketing

By the end of this book, readers will have gained a deep understanding of the strategies and principles that have shaped the field of marketing. They will be equipped with practical insights and actionable advice from the greatest minds in the industry, empowering them to create influential and successful marketing campaigns.

Marketing is an ever-evolving field that requires a blend of creativity, strategic thinking, and an understanding of human behavior. Masters of Influence - Lessons from America's Greatest Sales, Marketing, and Advertising Minds is a journey through the lives and legacies of the most influential figures in marketing history. Their stories, principles, and strategies provide a rich source of knowledge and inspiration for anyone looking to excel in the world of marketing. Whether you are a seasoned marketer or just starting out, this book offers valuable lessons that will help you harness the power of influence and achieve your marketing goals.

With Resilience and Hope,

Stephen Nalley

Contents

Acknowledgment: ii
About the Author: iii
Preface: iv

Chapter 1: Introduction

Chapter 2: David Ogilvy - The Father of Advertising

- Biography and career highlights
- Core principles and philosophies
- Key campaigns and their impact
- Lessons on copywriting and brand image
- Modern applications of Ogilvy's methods

Chapter 3: Philip Kotler - The Father of Modern Marketing

- Biography and contributions to marketing theory
- Evolution of marketing from Kotler's perspective
- Understanding consumer behavior and market segmentation
- The 4 Ps of Marketing (Product, Price, Place, Promotion)
- Applying Kotler's principles in the digital age

Chapter 4: Mary Kay Ash - Empowerment and Direct Sales

- Biography and the founding of Mary Kay

Cosmetics
- The philosophy of empowering women through sales
- The importance of personal connections in marketing
- Strategies for building a loyal salesforce and customer base
- Legacy and lasting impact on direct sales marketing

Chapter 5: Seth Godin - The Modern Marketing Guru

- Biography and key contributions to marketing
- Understanding permission marketing
- The concept of tribes and community building
- The importance of authenticity and storytelling
- Case studies of successful campaigns inspired by Godin's ideas

Chapter 6: Steve Jobs - The Art of Innovation and Branding

- Biography and impact on the technology industry
- Jobs' approach to product design and user experience
- The role of storytelling in Apple's marketing
- Key lessons from Apple's most iconic campaigns
- The importance of vision and leadership in branding

Chapter 7: Gary Vaynerchuk - Social Media and Digital Marketing

- Biography and rise to prominence
- The power of social media in modern marketing
- Content creation and personal branding strategies
- Engaging with audiences and building a community
- Tips for leveraging digital platforms to grow a brand

Chapter 8: Dan Kennedy - Direct Response Marketing

- Biography and career achievements
- The fundamentals of direct response marketing
- Techniques for crafting compelling offers
- Case studies of successful direct response campaigns
- Integrating direct response principles into broader marketing strategies

Chapter 9: Rosser Reeves - The Unique Selling Proposition

- Biography and key contributions to advertising
- Understanding the Unique Selling Proposition (USP)
- Creating and communicating a strong USP
- Case studies of campaigns featuring effective USPs
- Applying USP concepts to modern marketing challenges

Chapter 10: Claude Hopkins - Scientific Advertising

- Biography and career highlights
- The principles of scientific advertising
- The importance of testing and measuring results
- Techniques for writing effective copy
- Lessons from Hopkins' campaigns that remain relevant today

Chapter 11: Shaping the Future - Integrating Lessons from the Masters

- Synthesis of key lessons from each master
- Strategies for integrating these lessons into modern marketing
- Adapting to future marketing trends and challenges
- Building a legacy of influence and success in marketing

Page Left Blank Intentionally

Chapter 1:

Introduction:

The Power of Influence in Marketing

Marketing is the dynamic force that fuels the engine of commerce. It is the art of persuasion, the science of consumer behavior, and the craft of storytelling all rolled into one. The ability to influence and inspire action through marketing has been the cornerstone of successful businesses for centuries. Yet, in an era of rapid technological change and intense competition, mastering this craft has become more challenging and essential than ever. This book, "Masters of Influence - Lessons from America's Greatest Sales, Marketing, and Advertising Minds," is designed to provide a comprehensive guide for marketers, business leaders, and aspiring entrepreneurs who wish to elevate their skills by learning from the true legends of the field.

Overview of the Book's Purpose

The primary purpose of this book is to distill the wisdom and insights of America's most influential sales, marketing, and advertising minds. These individuals are not just historical figures; they are the architects of modern marketing practices, the innovators who have pushed the boundaries of what's possible. By studying their strategies, principles, and philosophies, readers can gain invaluable knowledge that can be applied to contemporary marketing challenges. Whether you are a seasoned marketer looking to refine your skills or a novice eager to learn the ropes, this book offers a treasure trove of insights that can help you navigate the complex and ever-evolving world of marketing.

This book is structured to provide a deep dive into the lives and careers of twelve marketing legends, each of whom has contributed significantly to the field in their unique ways. By understanding their approaches, campaigns, and the rationale behind their decisions, readers can extract practical lessons that are as relevant today as they were when these icons first implemented them. The goal is not merely to celebrate their achievements but to dissect and analyze their methods to uncover timeless principles that can drive success in any marketing endeavor.

Importance of Learning from the Masters

In any discipline, learning from the masters is a time-honored tradition. Just as aspiring artists study the works of Michelangelo and Picasso, and budding scientists delve into the theories of Einstein and Newton, marketers, too, can benefit immensely from understanding the techniques and philosophies of the industry's giants. The masters of marketing are those individuals who have consistently demonstrated an ability to influence and persuade on a grand scale, often with transformative effects on their respective companies and industries.

One of the key benefits of learning from the masters is the ability to stand on the shoulders of giants. By leveraging the knowledge and experience of those who have paved the way, you can avoid common pitfalls and accelerate your own learning curve. The masters have often faced and overcome challenges similar to those you might encounter, and their solutions can provide a roadmap for navigating similar obstacles.

Furthermore, studying the masters allows you to gain a broader perspective on what works and what doesn't in marketing. It exposes you to a diverse array of strategies and tactics, enabling you to build a more versatile and adaptable skill set. The insights gained from these legends can spark new ideas, inspire innovative approaches, and help you develop a more robust and effective marketing strategy.

Learning from the masters also instills a sense of humility and respect for the craft. It reminds us that marketing is not merely about following trends or mimicking popular tactics but about understanding the fundamental principles that drive human behavior and leveraging those principles to create meaningful connections with audiences.

Brief Introduction of the Key Figures to be Discussed

This book features an array of distinguished figures whose contributions to sales, marketing, and advertising are nothing short of legendary. Here is a brief introduction to the key figures whose insights and strategies we will explore in detail:

- David Ogilvy - Often referred to as the "Father of Advertising," Ogilvy's approach to copywriting and brand image revolutionized the industry. His emphasis on research, big ideas, and creative discipline set new standards for advertising excellence.

- Philip Kotler - Known as the "Father of Modern Marketing," Kotler's theories on consumer behavior, market segmentation, and the 4 Ps of marketing (Product, Price, Place, Promotion) have become foundational concepts in the field.

- Mary Kay Ash - Founder of Mary Kay Cosmetics, Ash built a direct sales empire by empowering women and emphasizing the importance of personal connections and customer service.

- Seth Godin - A modern marketing guru, Godin's concepts of permission marketing, tribes, and authenticity have reshaped the way marketers engage with their audiences in the digital age.

- Steve Jobs - The co-founder of Apple Inc., Jobs was a master of innovation and branding. His ability to create products that were not only functional but also aspirational set new benchmarks in the technology industry.

- Gary Vaynerchuk - A pioneer in social media and digital marketing, Vaynerchuk's strategies for content creation, personal branding, and

audience engagement have made him a leading voice in the industry.
- Dan Kennedy - An expert in direct response marketing, Kennedy's principles of crafting compelling offers and measuring results have helped countless businesses achieve measurable success.

- Rosser Reeves - Known for his development of the Unique Selling Proposition (USP), Reeves emphasized the importance of differentiating a product in a crowded marketplace.

- Claude Hopkins - A pioneer of scientific advertising, Hopkins' data-driven approach and emphasis on testing and measuring results have made him a lasting influence on the field.

- Jay Conrad Levinson - The creator of guerrilla marketing, Levinson introduced creative, low-cost marketing strategies that have become essential tools for small businesses.

- Al Ries and Jack Trout - Pioneers of the concept of positioning, Ries and Trout's work on brand strategy and differentiation has provided a framework for effective marketing in competitive markets.

Outline of What Readers Can Expect to Learn

By delving into the lives and careers of these marketing legends, readers will gain a comprehensive understanding of the principles and strategies that have shaped the industry. Here is an outline of what you can expect to learn from this book:

- Foundational Principles of Marketing - Learn the core concepts that underpin successful marketing strategies, from market segmentation to the 4 Ps.

- Innovative Approaches and Techniques - Discover the innovative approaches used by these masters to solve marketing challenges and achieve their goals.

- Real-World Applications - Explore case studies and examples of how these principles have been applied in real-world scenarios, providing practical insights that you can implement in your own marketing efforts.

- The Role of Creativity and Research - Understand the balance between creativity and research in crafting effective marketing campaigns.

- Building Strong Brands - Learn how to create and maintain a strong brand identity that resonates with your target audience.

- Effective Communication Strategies - Gain insights into the communication techniques used by these masters to convey their messages clearly and persuasively.

- Leveraging Technology and Digital Media - Discover how to harness the power of digital media and technology to enhance your marketing efforts and reach a broader audience.

- Empowering and Motivating Teams - Learn from the leadership styles and motivational techniques used by these legends to inspire their teams and achieve remarkable results.

- Adaptation and Continuous Improvement - Understand the importance of adapting to changes in the market and continuously improving your strategies to stay ahead of the competition.

- The Art of Storytelling - Explore the role of storytelling in marketing and how to craft compelling narratives that captivate and engage your audience.

- Measuring and Analyzing Success - Learn how to measure the success of your marketing efforts and use data to refine and optimize your strategies.

- Ethical Considerations in Marketing - Gain insights into the ethical considerations and responsibilities that come with the power to influence and persuade.

By the end of this book, you will have a deeper appreciation for the art and science of marketing and a toolkit of strategies and principles that you can apply to your own work. The lessons from these masters are not just historical anecdotes; they are timeless principles that continue to drive success in today's fast-paced and ever-changing marketing landscape.

Whether you are looking to build a strong brand, create compelling marketing campaigns, or simply understand the fundamentals of influence and persuasion, "Masters of Influence - Lessons from America's Greatest Sales, Marketing, and Advertising Minds" is your guide to becoming a master of influence in your own right.

Prepare to embark on a journey through the minds of marketing's greatest legends, and discover the secrets behind their success. Welcome to the world of masters of influence.

Chapter 2:

David Ogilvy The Father of Advertising

David Ogilvy was born on June 23, 1911, in West Horsley, Surrey, England, into a family of Scottish descent. His father, Francis John Longley Ogilvy, was a Gaelic-speaking Highlander who worked as a classical scholar and financial broker, while his mother, Dorothy Blew Fairfield, came from a prominent London family. Ogilvy's upbringing was marked by a blend of intellectual rigor and financial hardship, which would shape his tenacity and inventive spirit in later years.

Ogilvy's academic journey began at St Cyprian's School, Eastbourne, followed by a scholarship to Fettes College in Edinburgh, and later, he attended Christ Church, Oxford. However, his time at Oxford was short-lived, as he left the university without completing his degree. Ogilvy's early departure from formal education did not impede his intellectual development; instead, it fostered a practical and hands-on approach to learning and work.

Ogilvy's initial foray into the professional world was diverse and eclectic. He worked as a chef in Paris, a door-to-door stove salesman in Scotland, and even as a social worker in the slums of Edinburgh. These varied experiences equipped him with a unique understanding of human behavior, a trait that would later become invaluable in his advertising career.

The turning point in Ogilvy's career came when he joined the London advertising agency Mather & Crowther, where his brother worked. His assignment to write an instruction manual for door-to-door salesmen of AGA cookers would become legendary. The manual was so effective that Fortune magazine later called it "the finest sales instruction manual ever written." This early success in salesmanship highlighted Ogilvy's talent for persuasive communication and set the stage for his future in advertising.

Founding of Ogilvy & Mather

In 1938, seeking new opportunities, Ogilvy emigrated to the United States. His journey in the U.S. began at George Gallup's Audience Research Institute in New Jersey, where he gained a profound appreciation for the importance of research and data in understanding consumer behavior. This experience reinforced his belief in the power of knowledge and analytics in crafting effective advertising campaigns.

During World War II, Ogilvy worked for the British Intelligence Service at the British Embassy in Washington, D.C. This role further honed his skills in research and strategic thinking. After the war, Ogilvy moved to a farm in Lancaster County, Pennsylvania, where he lived a relatively quiet life as a farmer. However, the world of advertising was never far from his mind.

In 1948, with a modest sum of $6,000 and a belief in the untapped potential of the advertising industry, Ogilvy founded his own advertising agency, Hewitt, Ogilvy, Benson & Mather (later shortened to Ogilvy & Mather), in New York City. Despite having no clients and little experience running an agency, Ogilvy's conviction and vision for a new kind of advertising agency soon attracted attention.

Ogilvy's approach to advertising was revolutionary. He emphasized the importance of thorough research, the creation of compelling and intelligent copy, and a commitment to understanding the client's product inside and out. His belief in "advertising that sells" rather than just creative for creativity's sake set Ogilvy & Mather apart from its competitors. This philosophy quickly bore fruit, as the agency began to win significant accounts and grow its reputation.

Major Achievements and Accolades

Ogilvy's career is punctuated by numerous groundbreaking campaigns that not only garnered critical acclaim but also delivered substantial business results for his clients. Some of his most notable achievements include:

- The Hathaway Man: In 1951, Ogilvy created an iconic campaign for C.F. Hathaway Company, a small shirt manufacturer. The campaign featured a distinguished man with an eye patch, known as "The Hathaway Man." The eye patch was a last-minute addition by Ogilvy, intended to create intrigue and memorability. The campaign was a massive success, propelling Hathaway shirts into the national spotlight and exemplifying Ogilvy's knack for creating compelling brand stories.

- Rolls-Royce: Ogilvy's 1958 ad for Rolls-Royce is often cited as one of the greatest car advertisements of all time. The headline, "At 60 miles an hour the loudest noise in this new Rolls-Royce comes from the electric clock," combined with meticulous research and elegant copy, perfectly captured the luxury and precision of the brand. This ad not only boosted sales but also reinforced Rolls-Royce's image of unparalleled quality.

- Schweppes: Ogilvy's work with Schweppes introduced Americans to "Schweppervescence." Featuring Commander Edward Whitehead, the campaign used wit and sophistication to elevate the brand's status. The ads were so successful that Schweppes became synonymous with high-quality tonic water, cementing its place in the American market.

- Dove: In 1957, Ogilvy launched the Dove campaign, positioning it as "one-quarter moisturizing cream." This unique selling proposition helped differentiate Dove from other soaps, leading to a significant increase in market share. The campaign's emphasis on product benefits over extravagant claims became a hallmark of Ogilvy's approach.

- American Express: Ogilvy & Mather's long-running campaign for American Express, featuring the tagline "Don't leave home without it," is another testament to Ogilvy's brilliance. The campaign not only increased brand awareness but also fostered a sense of trust and reliability associated with the American Express card.

Throughout his career, Ogilvy received numerous accolades and recognition for his contributions to the advertising industry. In 1969, he was inducted into the American Advertising Federation Hall of Fame, solidifying his status as one of the industry's greats. His legacy is further immortalized in his seminal works, "Confessions of an Advertising Man" (1963) and "Ogilvy on Advertising" (1983), which remain essential reading for anyone in the field of marketing and advertising.

Ogilvy's influence extended beyond his campaigns. He was a champion of the creative process, advocating for the importance of art and copy working in harmony. He believed in the power of advertising to not only sell products but to elevate and enrich consumer experiences. His commitment to high standards, integrity, and a focus on results left an indelible mark on the industry.

Impact on Modern Advertising

David Ogilvy's legacy is not merely historical; his principles continue to resonate in today's advertising landscape. The emphasis on research, the power of a big idea, and the importance of understanding the consumer are more relevant than ever in an era where data-driven decision-making and consumer-centric marketing dominate.

Modern digital advertising owes much to Ogilvy's foundational principles. The use of analytics to understand consumer behavior, the focus on compelling and relevant content, and the integration of brand storytelling are all reflections of Ogilvy's influence. As digital platforms evolve, the core tenets of Ogilvy's approach provide a timeless framework for effective marketing.

Moreover, Ogilvy's belief in the potential of advertising to do more than just sell—to inform, entertain, and engage—has found new expression in content marketing, social media campaigns, and interactive brand experiences. His pioneering spirit and commitment to excellence continue to inspire marketers around the world to push the boundaries of creativity and effectiveness.

David Ogilvy's journey from a diverse and unconventional early career to becoming the "Father of Advertising" is a testament to his brilliance, creativity, and unwavering commitment to the craft. His ability to blend research with creativity, to craft compelling narratives that resonate with audiences, and to maintain a relentless focus on results has left an enduring legacy that continues to shape the advertising industry.

Ogilvy's story is not just one of professional success; it is a story of innovation, resilience, and a deep understanding of human behavior. By learning from his life and career, marketers today can gain valuable insights into what it takes to create impactful and memorable campaigns that stand the test of time.

As we delve deeper into the lives and lessons of other marketing legends in this book, Ogilvy's example will serve as a guiding light, illuminating the path to mastering the art of influence in marketing. His legacy reminds us that at its best, advertising is a powerful tool that can inspire, inform, and transform, leaving a lasting impact on both businesses and consumers alike.

Ogilvy's Core Principles and Philosophies

David Ogilvy, often hailed as the "Father of Advertising," established a legacy rooted in a set of core principles and philosophies that revolutionized the advertising industry. His emphasis on research, big ideas, and creative discipline formed the bedrock of his approach to advertising. These principles not only guided Ogilvy's own work but also influenced generations of marketers and advertisers who followed in his footsteps. In this section, we will delve deeply into these foundational elements of Ogilvy's philosophy and examine how they shaped some of his most iconic campaigns.

Importance of Research

One of Ogilvy's most enduring legacies is his unwavering belief in the importance of research. He once famously said, "Advertising people who ignore research are as dangerous as generals who ignore decodes of enemy signals." For Ogilvy, research was not a mere adjunct to the creative process; it was the foundation upon which successful advertising campaigns were built.

Consumer Understanding

At the heart of Ogilvy's research-driven approach was a profound commitment to understanding the consumer. Ogilvy believed that effective advertising required a deep empathy with the consumer's needs, desires, and behaviors. This understanding could only be achieved through rigorous research. He advocated for the use of quantitative data to uncover insights about consumer preferences and buying habits. This approach helped him to craft messages that resonated deeply with the target audience.

For instance, in his work with Rolls-Royce, Ogilvy's team conducted extensive research to understand the affluent customers who were likely to buy the luxury car. They discovered that these customers valued precision and quietness, leading to the creation of the famous headline: "At 60 miles an hour the loudest noise in this new Rolls-Royce comes from the electric clock." This insight, rooted in research, was instrumental in crafting a message that appealed directly to the desires of Rolls-Royce's target market.

Product Knowledge

Ogilvy also placed great importance on thorough product knowledge. He believed that it was essential for advertisers to become intimately familiar with the products they were promoting. This knowledge allowed them to highlight the most compelling features and benefits in their advertisements. Ogilvy's dedication to product research was evident in his meticulous approach to writing copy. He would often spend weeks studying a product, interviewing engineers, and understanding every detail before crafting his ads.

In the case of Hathaway Shirts, Ogilvy's research revealed the superior quality and craftsmanship of the shirts. This understanding informed the creative direction of the campaign, which featured the distinguished "man in the eyepatch" wearing Hathaway's premium shirts. The campaign's success can be attributed to Ogilvy's deep understanding of the product and his ability to communicate its unique qualities effectively.

Pre-Testing and Feedback

Ogilvy was also a strong proponent of pre-testing advertising concepts before launching them. He believed that testing could provide valuable feedback and help refine the messaging to ensure maximum impact. This approach was particularly evident in his work with television commercials, where he would often test different versions of an ad to determine which one resonated best with the audience.

By incorporating research at every stage of the advertising process, Ogilvy was able to create campaigns that were not only creative but also highly effective. His commitment to research ensured that his ads were grounded in reality and aligned with consumer needs, resulting in messages that were both persuasive and memorable.

Focus on Big Ideas

Another cornerstone of Ogilvy's philosophy was his focus on big ideas. He believed that the most successful advertisements were those that were built around a single, powerful idea. This idea, or "big idea," as Ogilvy called it, was the driving force behind the creative execution and the key to capturing the audience's attention.

Simplicity and Clarity

Ogilvy's big ideas were often characterized by their simplicity and clarity. He understood that in a cluttered advertising landscape, it was essential to cut through the noise with a clear and compelling message. His emphasis on simplicity was not about dumbing down the message but about distilling it to its most potent form. This clarity allowed the big idea to shine through and resonate with the audience.

For example, the big idea behind the Rolls-Royce campaign was encapsulated in the headline: "At 60 miles an hour the loudest noise in this new Rolls-Royce comes from the electric clock." This simple yet powerful statement highlighted the precision and luxury of the car in a way that was immediately understandable and impactful.

Emotional Appeal

Ogilvy also recognized the importance of emotional appeal in advertising. He believed that big ideas needed to evoke an emotional response from the audience. This emotional connection was what made the message memorable and persuasive. Whether it was the sophistication and intrigue of the Hathaway Man or the elegance and refinement of Schweppes, Ogilvy's campaigns were designed to evoke specific emotions that aligned with the brand's identity and values.

The Hathaway Shirts campaign, featuring the man with the eyepatch, is a prime example of this approach. The eyepatch added an element of mystery and sophistication, appealing to the audience's desire for elegance and distinction. This emotional appeal was a key factor in the campaign's success and its ability to elevate Hathaway shirts to a symbol of refined taste.

Differentiation

A crucial aspect of Ogilvy's focus on big ideas was differentiation. He believed that a strong advertising campaign needed to set the brand apart from its competitors. The big idea was often the differentiating factor that highlighted the unique qualities of the product or service. By focusing on what made the brand special, Ogilvy's campaigns were able to create a distinct and memorable identity for the brand.

In the case of Schweppes, the big idea was encapsulated in the concept of "Schweppervescence." This idea not only highlighted the unique effervescence of the beverage but also positioned it as a sophisticated and high-quality product. The campaign's success lay in its ability to differentiate Schweppes from other tonic waters and create a lasting impression in the minds of consumers.

Longevity

Ogilvy's big ideas were not just about creating a momentary impact; they were designed for longevity. He believed that a strong idea should have the potential to sustain a campaign over time and continue to resonate with the audience. This approach ensured that the brand's messaging remained consistent and effective across different media and over extended periods.

The longevity of the "Don't leave home without it" campaign for American Express is a testament to the enduring power of Ogilvy's big ideas. This campaign ran for several decades, reinforcing the brand's promise of security and reliability. The consistency and longevity of the message helped build strong brand equity and consumer trust.

Creative Discipline

Ogilvy's approach to advertising was characterized by a unique blend of creativity and discipline. He believed that creativity needed to be harnessed and directed by a disciplined process to achieve the best results. This creative discipline was evident in every aspect of his work, from copywriting to design to strategic planning.

Copywriting Excellence

Ogilvy was a master of copywriting, and his disciplined approach to crafting copy set a new standard in the industry. He believed that every word in an advertisement needed to serve a purpose and contribute to the overall message. His copy was known for its clarity, precision, and persuasive power.

One of the hallmarks of Ogilvy's copywriting was his use of long-form copy. He believed that if a product was worth buying, it was worth explaining in detail. His ads often featured extensive copy that provided comprehensive information about the product's features and benefits. This approach not only informed the consumer but also built trust and credibility.

For example, the Rolls-Royce ad included detailed descriptions of the car's features, such as the engineering precision and the luxurious interior. This attention to detail demonstrated Ogilvy's commitment to providing valuable information to the consumer and reinforced the brand's image of quality and sophistication.

Visual Impact

While Ogilvy placed great importance on copy, he also understood the power of visual impact. He believed that the visual elements of an advertisement needed to complement and enhance the message. This meant that every visual detail, from the layout to the typography to the imagery, needed to be carefully considered and executed with precision.

In the Hathaway Shirts campaign, the use of a distinguished man with an eyepatch created a strong visual impact that captured the audience's attention. The clean and elegant design of the ads reinforced the brand's image of sophistication and quality. Ogilvy's disciplined approach to visual design ensured that the visuals worked in harmony with the copy to create a cohesive and compelling message.

Strategic Planning

Ogilvy's creative discipline extended to strategic planning as well. He believed that a successful advertising campaign needed to be grounded in a solid strategic framework. This involved setting clear objectives, identifying the target audience, and developing a coherent strategy to achieve the desired outcomes.

Ogilvy's strategic planning was evident in his approach to the Schweppes campaign. He recognized that the target audience for Schweppes was sophisticated and discerning consumers. The campaign's strategy was to position Schweppes as a premium beverage that appealed to this audience's refined tastes. The use of Commander Edward Whitehead, with his British accent and dignified demeanor, reinforced this positioning and aligned with the strategic objectives.

Consistency and Integrity

A key aspect of Ogilvy's creative discipline was his commitment to consistency and integrity. He believed that a brand's messaging needed to be consistent across all touchpoints to build a strong and cohesive brand identity. This consistency extended to the tone, style, and content of the ads.

Ogilvy also emphasized the importance of integrity in advertising. He believed that honesty and transparency were essential for building trust with the consumer. His ads were known for their straightforward and truthful messaging, avoiding exaggerated claims and gimmicks. This integrity helped build long-term relationships with consumers and established Ogilvy as a trusted and respected figure in the industry.

Key Campaigns and Their Impact

David Ogilvy's career is punctuated by a series of iconic campaigns that not only garnered critical acclaim but also delivered substantial business results for his clients. These campaigns are a testament to his core principles and philosophies, demonstrating the power of research, big ideas, and creative discipline in creating effective and memorable advertising. In this section, we will examine three of Ogilvy's most celebrated campaigns: Rolls-Royce, Hathaway Shirts, and Schweppes.

Rolls-Royce: "At 60 miles an hour the loudest noise in this new Rolls-Royce comes from the electric clock."

The Rolls-Royce campaign, launched in 1958, is often cited as one of the greatest car advertisements of all time. The ad's headline, "At 60 miles an hour the loudest noise in this new Rolls-Royce comes from the electric clock," is a masterclass in Ogilvy's approach to advertising.

Research and Insight

The genesis of the Rolls-Royce campaign lies in Ogilvy's commitment to research. Ogilvy and his team conducted extensive research to understand the affluent customers who were likely to buy a Rolls-Royce. They discovered that these customers valued precision, luxury, and quietness. This insight was the foundation for the campaign's big idea.

The research also involved a detailed study of the car's engineering and design. Ogilvy's team interviewed Rolls-Royce engineers and spent time understanding the car's features and benefits. This thorough product knowledge allowed them to craft a message that highlighted the car's unique qualities in a compelling and memorable way.

The Big Idea

The big idea behind the Rolls-Royce campaign was to emphasize the car's extraordinary quietness and precision. The headline, "At 60 miles an hour the loudest noise in this new Rolls-Royce comes from the electric clock," perfectly encapsulated this idea. It was a simple yet powerful statement that conveyed the car's luxury and refinement in a way that was immediately understandable and impactful.

The headline was supported by detailed copy that provided further information about the car's features, such as the precision engineering, luxurious interior, and attention to detail. This combination of a strong headline and informative copy demonstrated Ogilvy's belief in the power of long-form copy and his commitment to providing valuable information to the consumer.

Visual Execution

The visual elements of the Rolls-Royce ad were carefully designed to complement the headline and reinforce the message. The ad featured a striking photograph of the car, highlighting its elegant design and luxurious features. The clean and sophisticated layout of the ad reflected the car's image of quality and refinement.

Impact and Legacy

The Rolls-Royce campaign was a resounding success, boosting sales and reinforcing the brand's image of unparalleled quality and luxury. The ad's impact extended beyond the immediate sales results; it also cemented Rolls-Royce's position as a symbol of prestige and excellence.

The campaign's success can be attributed to Ogilvy's core principles of research, big ideas, and creative discipline. By understanding the consumer's needs, crafting a powerful and memorable message, and executing it with precision and consistency, Ogilvy created a campaign that stands as a benchmark for effective advertising.

Hathaway Shirts: The Man in the Eyepatch

The Hathaway Shirts campaign, launched in 1951, is another iconic example of Ogilvy's genius. The campaign featured a distinguished man wearing an eyepatch, known as "The Hathaway Man," and became a symbol of sophistication and quality.

Research and Insight

As with the Rolls-Royce campaign, the Hathaway Shirts campaign was grounded in thorough research. Ogilvy's team conducted extensive research to understand the market for high-quality shirts and the preferences of the target audience. They discovered that the audience valued sophistication, elegance, and craftsmanship.

The research also involved a detailed study of Hathaway's products. Ogilvy's team examined the quality of the shirts, the materials used, and the craftsmanship involved in their production. This deep understanding of the product informed the creative direction of the campaign and allowed them to highlight the unique qualities of Hathaway shirts.

The Big Idea

The big idea behind the Hathaway Shirts campaign was to create a distinctive and memorable brand image that conveyed sophistication and quality. The use of the eyepatch was a stroke of creative genius. It added an element of mystery and intrigue, making "The Hathaway Man" instantly recognizable and memorable.

The eyepatch was not part of the original plan; it was a last-minute addition by Ogilvy. He believed that it would create a unique and memorable image that would capture the audience's attention. This intuition proved to be correct, as the eyepatch became the defining feature of the campaign.

Visual Execution

The visual elements of the Hathaway Shirts campaign were critical to its success. The ads featured "The Hathaway Man" in various sophisticated settings, wearing the premium shirts. The clean and elegant design of the ads reinforced the brand's image of quality and refinement.

The use of high-quality photography and meticulous attention to detail in the visual execution demonstrated Ogilvy's creative discipline. Every visual element was carefully considered and designed to enhance the overall message of sophistication and elegance.

Impact and Legacy

The Hathaway Shirts campaign was a tremendous success, propelling the brand into the national spotlight and significantly boosting sales. The campaign's impact extended beyond the immediate business results; it also established Hathaway shirts as a symbol of refined taste and quality.

The success of the campaign can be attributed to Ogilvy's core principles of research, big ideas, and creative discipline. By understanding the market and the product, crafting a distinctive and memorable brand image, and executing it with precision and consistency, Ogilvy created a campaign that stands as a testament to the power of effective advertising.

Schweppes: "Schweppervescence"

The Schweppes campaign, launched in the 1950s, is another iconic example of Ogilvy's brilliance. The campaign introduced Americans to the concept of "Schweppervescence" and positioned Schweppes as a sophisticated and high-quality tonic water.

Research and Insight

The Schweppes campaign was grounded in extensive research. Ogilvy's team conducted research to understand the market for tonic water and the preferences of the target audience. They discovered that the audience valued sophistication and quality, and were willing to pay a premium for a superior product.

The research also involved a detailed study of Schweppes' products. Ogilvy's team examined the unique qualities of Schweppes tonic water, including its distinctive effervescence. This deep understanding of the product informed the creative direction of the campaign and allowed them to highlight its unique qualities effectively.

The Big Idea

The big idea behind the Schweppes campaign was encapsulated in the concept of "Schweppervescence." This idea highlighted the unique effervescence of the beverage and positioned it as a sophisticated and high-quality product. The use of the term "Schweppervescence" added an element of intrigue and sophistication, making the brand instantly recognizable and memorable.

The campaign featured Commander Edward Whitehead, a distinguished British gentleman with a dignified demeanor. Whitehead's persona added an element of sophistication and elegance to the brand, reinforcing its image of quality and refinement.

Visual Execution

The visual elements of the Schweppes campaign were critical to its success. The ads featured Commander Whitehead in various sophisticated settings, often enjoying a glass of Schweppes. The clean and elegant design of the ads reinforced the brand's image of sophistication and quality.

The use of high-quality photography and meticulous attention to detail in the visual execution demonstrated Ogilvy's creative discipline. Every visual element was carefully considered and designed to enhance the overall message of sophistication and elegance.

Impact and Legacy

The Schweppes campaign was a tremendous success, significantly boosting sales and establishing Schweppes as a premium brand in the American market. The campaign's impact extended beyond the immediate business results; it also cemented Schweppes' position as a symbol of sophistication and quality.

The success of the campaign can be attributed to

Ogilvy's core principles of research, big ideas, and creative discipline. By understanding the market and the product, crafting a distinctive and memorable brand image, and executing it with precision and consistency, Ogilvy created a campaign that stands as a testament to the power of effective advertising.
Conclusion

David Ogilvy's core principles and philosophies of research, big ideas, and creative discipline have left an indelible mark on the advertising industry. His campaigns for Rolls-Royce, Hathaway Shirts, and Schweppes are not just examples of brilliant advertising; they are case studies in the application of his principles to create memorable and effective messages that resonate with consumers.

Ogilvy's commitment to understanding the consumer, crafting compelling and distinctive messages, and executing them with precision and consistency has set a standard for excellence in advertising. His legacy continues to inspire and guide marketers and advertisers around the world, reminding us that at its best, advertising is a powerful tool that can inform, entertain, and transform. By learning from Ogilvy's principles and applying them to our own work, we can create advertising that not only sells products but also builds brands and connects with audiences in meaningful and lasting ways.

Lessons on Copywriting and Brand Image

David Ogilvy's mastery of copywriting and brand image has left a profound legacy in the advertising world. His meticulous approach to crafting compelling copy, building a strong brand image, and maintaining consistency in messaging continues to influence modern marketers. This section delves into these foundational aspects of Ogilvy's work and explores their application in contemporary contexts. Crafting Compelling Copy

Ogilvy believed that copywriting was the heart of advertising. He viewed the written word as the primary vehicle for conveying the message and persuading the audience. Here are some of his key lessons on crafting compelling copy:

Understand the Product and Audience

One of Ogilvy's fundamental tenets was the necessity of understanding both the product and the audience. He spent considerable time researching the products he advertised, ensuring he knew every detail. This deep product knowledge allowed him to write copy that was both informative and persuasive.

Similarly, understanding the audience was crucial. Ogilvy believed that to write compelling copy, one must get into the minds of the consumers, understand their desires, fears, and motivations. This empathy enabled him to create messages that resonated deeply with the target audience.

Focus on Benefits, Not Features

Ogilvy emphasized the importance of focusing on benefits rather than features. While features describe the product, benefits explain how those features will improve the consumer's life. For example, instead of merely stating that a car has a powerful engine, Ogilvy would highlight the benefits of that engine – such as speed, reliability, and safety.

In his Rolls-Royce campaign, Ogilvy didn't just list the car's features. He used the iconic headline, "At 60 miles an hour the loudest noise in this new Rolls-Royce comes from the electric clock," to convey the benefit of quietness, a feature highly valued by luxury car buyers.

Clarity and Simplicity

Ogilvy's copy was renowned for its clarity and simplicity. He avoided jargon and complicated language, opting instead for straightforward, conversational tones. His philosophy was that the best copy is simple enough for a child to understand yet sophisticated enough to engage an adult.

This principle is evident in his famous ad for Dove soap, which stated, "Only Dove is one-quarter moisturizing cream." The message was clear, concise, and immediately understandable, making it easy for consumers to grasp the product's unique selling proposition.

Storytelling

Ogilvy was a master storyteller. He understood that humans are naturally drawn to stories and that a well-told story could make an advertisement more engaging and memorable. Whether through a character like "The Hathaway Man" or a narrative about the product's creation, Ogilvy's ads often told stories that captivated the audience.

The "Hathaway Man" campaign is a prime example. By creating a mysterious character with an eyepatch, Ogilvy wove a narrative that intrigued consumers and added an element of sophistication and allure to the Hathaway brand.

Use of Headlines

Ogilvy placed significant importance on headlines, often stating that if the headline didn't capture the reader's attention, the rest of the ad was wasted. He believed that a good headline could increase readership and engagement by a significant margin.

His headlines were not only attention-grabbing but also informative. For example, the headline for his Rolls-Royce ad immediately conveyed the car's superior quietness, setting the stage for the rest of the ad to provide more detailed information.

Testing and Revision

Ogilvy was a firm believer in testing and revising copy. He often tested different versions of an ad to see which one performed best and wasn't afraid to revise his work based on feedback. This iterative process ensured that the final copy was as effective as possible.

By adhering to these principles, Ogilvy crafted compelling copy that not only captured attention but also persuaded and converted. His ability to combine creativity with strategic thinking made his copywriting exceptionally effective.

Building a Strong Brand Image

Ogilvy understood that a strong brand image was essential for long-term success. He believed that advertising should not only drive sales but also build a lasting brand identity. Here are some of his key lessons on building a strong brand image:

Consistency in Branding

Ogilvy emphasized the importance of consistency in branding. He believed that every piece of communication should reinforce the brand's identity, ensuring a cohesive and recognizable image. This consistency helps build trust and loyalty among consumers.

For example, in his work with Schweppes, Ogilvy consistently used the image of Commander Edward Whitehead, the sophisticated British gentleman, to convey the brand's high-quality and refined nature. This consistent portrayal helped solidify Schweppes' image in the minds of consumers.

Distinctive Identity

Creating a distinctive identity was another key aspect of Ogilvy's approach to branding. He believed that a brand needed to stand out from the competition and have a unique personality. This distinctive identity could be achieved through various elements, including logos, color schemes, and brand messaging.

Ogilvy's "Hathaway Man" campaign is a testament to

this principle. By using the eyepatch as a distinctive visual element, he created a memorable and unique brand identity that set Hathaway shirts apart from competitors.

Emotional Connection

Ogilvy understood the power of emotional connections in building a strong brand image. He believed that brands needed to resonate emotionally with consumers to create lasting loyalty. This emotional connection could be achieved through storytelling, relatable characters, and addressing consumers' desires and aspirations.

The Dove campaign, with its focus on moisturizing and caring for the skin, created an emotional connection with consumers who valued self-care and health. This emotional appeal helped Dove build a loyal customer base.

Quality and Credibility

Ogilvy believed that a strong brand image was built on quality and credibility. He emphasized the importance of delivering high-quality products and ensuring that advertising messages were honest and credible. This commitment to quality and credibility helped build trust with consumers.

For example, Ogilvy's meticulous research and attention to detail in the Rolls-Royce campaign ensured that the claims made in the ad were credible and backed by evidence. This honesty helped reinforce the brand's image of luxury and reliability.

Long-Term Vision

Ogilvy advocated for a long-term vision in branding. He believed that building a strong brand image required sustained effort over time and that brands should not sacrifice long-term equity for short-term gains. This long-term perspective ensured that the brand's identity remained strong and relevant.

Ogilvy's work with American Express is an example of this long-term vision. The "Don't leave home without it" campaign ran for several decades, reinforcing the brand's promise of security and reliability and building strong brand equity over time.
Consistency in Messaging

Consistency in messaging is a hallmark of Ogilvy's approach to advertising. He believed that maintaining a consistent message across all touchpoints was essential for building a strong brand image and ensuring effective communication. Here are some of his key lessons on consistency in messaging:

Unified Voice and Tone

Ogilvy emphasized the importance of maintaining a unified voice and tone in all communications. Whether it was print ads, TV commercials, or other forms of media, the brand's voice and tone needed to be consistent to create a cohesive identity.

For example, the tone of the Rolls-Royce ads was always sophisticated and refined, reflecting the brand's luxury image. This consistent tone helped reinforce the brand's identity and made the messaging more effective.

Reinforcing Key Messages

Ogilvy believed that key messages needed to be consistently reinforced to ensure they were remembered by the audience. Repetition of core messages helped embed them in the consumer's mind and build strong brand associations.

The "Schweppervescence" campaign consistently reinforced the idea of sophistication and high quality, making Schweppes synonymous with these attributes. This consistent reinforcement helped build a strong and memorable brand image.

Aligning with Brand Values

Consistency in messaging also meant aligning all communications with the brand's values. Ogilvy believed that every piece of communication should reflect the brand's core values and mission, ensuring authenticity and credibility.

The Dove campaign consistently aligned with the brand's values of self-care and health, reinforcing the brand's commitment to these principles. This alignment helped build trust and loyalty among consumers.

Cross-Channel Consistency

Ogilvy recognized the importance of maintaining consistency across different channels and platforms. Whether it was print, TV, radio, or digital media, the brand's message needed to be consistent to create a cohesive and recognizable identity.

In the case of American Express, the "Don't leave home without it" message was consistently used across various media, from print ads to TV commercials. This cross-channel consistency helped build strong brand recognition and reinforced the brand's promise.

Adaptability within Consistency

While consistency was crucial, Ogilvy also understood the need for adaptability. He believed that the core message should remain consistent, but the execution could be adapted to suit different contexts and audiences. This adaptability ensured that the message remained relevant and effective across different situations.

For example, the Rolls-Royce campaign maintained a consistent message of luxury and precision, but the execution varied depending on the medium and audience. This adaptability within consistency helped ensure the message resonated with different segments of the target audience.

Modern Applications of Ogilvy's Methods

David Ogilvy's principles and methods have stood the test of time and continue to influence modern marketing practices. In today's digital age, these principles have been adapted to suit new media and evolving consumer behaviors. This section explores the modern applications of Ogilvy's methods in digital adaptations, social media campaigns, and brand storytelling in the 21st century.

Digital Adaptations

The rise of digital media has transformed the advertising landscape, creating new opportunities and challenges for marketers. Ogilvy's principles, however, remain relevant and provide a solid foundation for effective digital advertising.

Data-Driven Marketing

Ogilvy's emphasis on research and data is particularly relevant in the digital age. The vast amount of data available through digital channels allows marketers to gain deeper insights into consumer behavior and preferences. This data-driven approach enables more targeted and personalized advertising, improving effectiveness and ROI.

For example, digital marketers can use data analytics to segment their audience and tailor messages to specific groups, much like Ogilvy's approach to understanding the consumer. This targeted approach ensures that the right message reaches the right audience at the right time.

SEO and Content Marketing

Ogilvy's focus on compelling copy and informative content translates well to SEO and content marketing. Creating high-quality, valuable content that resonates with the audience is essential for improving search engine rankings and driving organic traffic.

Content marketing strategies that align with Ogilvy's principles include creating informative blog posts, engaging videos, and detailed product descriptions that provide real value to the consumer. This approach not only improves SEO but also builds trust and credibility with the audience.

Email Marketing

Email marketing is another area where Ogilvy's methods are highly applicable. Crafting compelling email copy that captures attention and drives action requires a deep understanding of the audience and a focus on benefits rather than features.

Ogilvy's emphasis on testing and revising copy is particularly relevant in email marketing. A/B testing different email variations can provide valuable insights into what resonates with the audience, allowing marketers to refine their messages for maximum impact.

Programmatic Advertising

Programmatic advertising, which uses automated technology to buy and place ads, benefits from Ogilvy's data-driven approach. By leveraging data to target specific audiences and optimize ad placements, programmatic advertising can achieve higher efficiency and effectiveness.

Ogilvy's principles of research and testing are integral to programmatic advertising. Continuous monitoring and optimization ensure that the ads perform well and deliver the desired results.

Social Media Campaigns

Social media has become a dominant force in modern marketing, offering unique opportunities for engagement and brand building. Ogilvy's principles provide valuable guidance for creating effective social media campaigns.

Engaging Content

Ogilvy's focus on compelling copy and storytelling is highly relevant on social media platforms. Creating engaging content that captures attention and encourages interaction is essential for success on social media.

For example, brands can use Ogilvy's storytelling techniques to create compelling narratives that resonate with their audience. Whether through posts, videos, or stories, engaging content that tells a story can build emotional connections and drive engagement.

Consistency in Branding

Maintaining consistency in branding across social media channels is crucial for building a strong brand image. Ogilvy's emphasis on a unified voice and tone ensures that the brand's identity remains cohesive and recognizable.

Brands can achieve consistency by using the same visual elements, tone of voice, and messaging across their social media profiles. This consistency helps build trust and familiarity with the audience.

Influencer Marketing

Influencer marketing leverages the reach and credibility of influencers to promote products and services. Ogilvy's principles of building emotional connections and leveraging distinctive identities align well with influencer marketing strategies.

By collaborating with influencers who align with the brand's values and identity, marketers can create authentic and engaging campaigns. These collaborations should focus on storytelling and highlighting the benefits of the product in a relatable and compelling way.

Social Listening and Engagement

Ogilvy's emphasis on understanding the consumer is particularly relevant in social listening and engagement. By monitoring social media conversations and engaging with the audience, brands can gain valuable insights and build stronger relationships.

Social listening tools allow marketers to track mentions, comments, and feedback, providing a deeper understanding of consumer sentiment. Engaging with the audience through responses and interactions helps build trust and loyalty.

Paid Social Advertising

Paid social advertising benefits from Ogilvy's principles of research and testing. By using data to target specific audiences and optimize ad placements, brands can achieve higher relevance and effectiveness.

A/B testing different ad variations and monitoring performance metrics allows marketers to refine their strategies and improve results. This data-driven approach ensures that paid social campaigns deliver maximum impact.

Brand Storytelling in the 21st Century

Brand storytelling has become a powerful tool for building emotional connections and creating memorable brand experiences. Ogilvy's mastery of storytelling provides valuable lessons for modern marketers.

Authenticity and Transparency

Ogilvy's commitment to honesty and credibility is particularly relevant in brand storytelling. Consumers today value authenticity and transparency, and brands that tell genuine and honest stories build stronger connections with their audience.

Authentic storytelling involves sharing real experiences, values, and mission in a way that resonates with consumers. This approach builds trust and fosters a deeper emotional connection.

Purpose-Driven Marketing

Purpose-driven marketing aligns with Ogilvy's principles of building a strong brand image based on values. Brands that communicate a clear purpose and mission can create more meaningful connections with their audience.

For example, brands that focus on sustainability, social responsibility, or community engagement can use storytelling to highlight their efforts and impact. This purpose-driven approach not only differentiates the brand but also builds loyalty and advocacy.

Interactive and Immersive Experiences

Advancements in technology have enabled more interactive and immersive storytelling experiences. Ogilvy's emphasis on engaging and memorable content translates well to these new formats.

Brands can use virtual reality (VR), augmented reality (AR), and interactive content to create immersive brand experiences. These experiences allow consumers to engage with the brand in unique and memorable ways, enhancing the overall impact of the storytelling.

User-Generated Content

User-generated content (UGC) leverages the power of consumer stories and experiences. Ogilvy's principles of emotional connection and relatability align well with UGC strategies.

Encouraging consumers to share their own stories and experiences with the brand creates authentic and relatable content. This approach not only builds trust but also fosters a sense of community and belonging.

Consistent Brand Narrative

Maintaining a consistent brand narrative across all touchpoints is essential for effective storytelling. Ogilvy's emphasis on consistency ensures that the brand's story remains cohesive and recognizable.

A consistent brand narrative involves aligning all communications with the brand's values, mission, and identity. This consistency builds a strong and memorable brand image that resonates with consumers.

David Ogilvy's principles and methods have left an enduring legacy in the advertising world. His lessons on crafting compelling copy, building a strong brand image, and maintaining consistency in messaging continue to guide modern marketers. In today's digital age, these principles have been adapted to suit new media and evolving consumer behaviors.

Digital adaptations, social media campaigns, and brand storytelling in the 21st century all benefit from Ogilvy's foundational principles. By understanding the consumer, focusing on benefits, and creating engaging and consistent messages, marketers can achieve greater impact and build stronger brands.

Ogilvy's legacy reminds us that effective advertising is both an art and a science. It requires creativity, strategic thinking, and a deep understanding of the audience. By learning from Ogilvy's principles and applying them to modern contexts, marketers can create advertising that not only sells products but also builds lasting connections with consumers.

Chapter 3:

Philip Kotler
The Marketing Guru

Philip Kotler, often revered as the "Father of Modern Marketing," has profoundly shaped the field of marketing through his extensive academic work, numerous publications, and groundbreaking theories. His contributions have not only defined marketing as a discipline but also transformed how businesses understand and engage with their markets. This section explores Kotler's biography, his key publications and theories, and the recognition and awards he has garnered throughout his illustrious career.

Academic Background and Early Influences

Philip Kotler was born on May 27, 1931, in Chicago, Illinois. His early life was marked by a keen interest in economics and social sciences, which would later form the foundation of his contributions to marketing. Kotler pursued his undergraduate studies at DePaul University, where he earned a degree in economics in 1953. His passion for understanding economic systems and consumer behavior led him to further his education at the University of Chicago, where he completed his master's degree in economics in 1956.

Kotler's academic journey did not stop there. He went

on to earn his Ph.D. in economics from the Massachusetts Institute of Technology (MIT) in 1959. At MIT, Kotler was influenced by some of the leading economists of the time, including Paul Samuelson and Robert Solow. These early influences instilled in him a rigorous analytical approach and a deep appreciation for the interplay between economics and marketing.

After completing his Ph.D., Kotler accepted a teaching position at Northwestern University's Kellogg School of Management in 1962. It was here that he began to develop his groundbreaking ideas on marketing. At Kellogg, Kotler was surrounded by a vibrant intellectual environment that encouraged innovation and interdisciplinary research. His background in economics provided a unique lens through which he viewed marketing, leading him to explore the economic underpinnings of consumer behavior and market dynamics.

Key Publications and Theories

Philip Kotler's contributions to marketing theory are extensive and varied, encompassing a wide range of topics from consumer behavior to strategic marketing. His work has been instrumental in shaping modern marketing practices and has provided a theoretical foundation for countless marketing professionals and academics. Some of his key publications and theories include:

1. Marketing Management: Analysis, Planning, and Control

First published in 1967, "Marketing Management:

Analysis, Planning, and Control" is arguably Kotler's most influential work. This seminal textbook has been translated into more than 20 languages and is widely used in business schools around the world. The book introduced a comprehensive framework for understanding and implementing marketing strategies, emphasizing the importance of a customer-centric approach.

In "Marketing Management," Kotler presented the idea that marketing should not be viewed merely as a function within a company, but as a critical process that involves analyzing market opportunities, planning and implementing marketing strategies, and controlling marketing activities. The book's detailed exploration of the 4 Ps of Marketing (Product, Price, Place, Promotion) provided a structured approach to developing effective marketing plans.

2. The Concept of Market Segmentation

Kotler's work on market segmentation revolutionized the way businesses approach their target markets. He argued that markets are not homogeneous and that consumers have diverse needs and preferences. By segmenting the market into distinct groups with similar characteristics, companies can tailor their marketing efforts to better meet the specific needs of each segment.

This concept of market segmentation has become a fundamental principle in marketing, enabling companies to create more targeted and effective marketing campaigns. Kotler's insights into segmentation have been particularly valuable in the development of niche marketing strategies and personalized marketing approaches.

3. Societal Marketing Concept

In the early 1970s, Kotler introduced the societal marketing concept, which expanded the traditional marketing framework to include the consideration of social and ethical implications. He argued that companies should not only focus on satisfying customer needs but also consider the broader impact of their activities on society and the environment.

The societal marketing concept emphasizes the importance of corporate social responsibility (CSR) and sustainable business practices. Kotler's advocacy for this approach has influenced many companies to adopt more socially responsible marketing strategies, balancing profitability with ethical considerations.

4. Marketing 3.0: From Products to Customers to the Human Spirit

In "Marketing 3.0: From Products to Customers to the Human Spirit," co-authored with Hermawan Kartajaya and Iwan Setiawan, Kotler explored the evolution of marketing in the digital age. Published in 2010, the book introduced the idea that marketing has moved beyond simply selling products and services to addressing the needs and aspirations of the human spirit.

Kotler argued that modern consumers are looking for more than just functional benefits; they seek brands that align with their values and contribute to their overall well-being. "Marketing 3.0" emphasized the importance of emotional engagement, authenticity, and purpose-driven marketing. This forward-thinking perspective has been particularly relevant in the age of social media and digital marketing, where consumers are more connected and informed than ever before.

5. Strategic Marketing for Nonprofit Organizations

Kotler's work has not been limited to the corporate sector; he has also made significant contributions to the field of nonprofit marketing. In "Strategic Marketing for Nonprofit Organizations," co-authored with Alan Andreasen, Kotler applied marketing principles to the unique challenges faced by nonprofit organizations.

The book provided a comprehensive framework for nonprofit marketing, including strategies for fundraising, advocacy, and stakeholder engagement. Kotler's insights have helped many nonprofit organizations adopt more effective marketing practices, enhancing their ability to achieve their missions and create social impact.
Recognition and Awards

Philip Kotler's contributions to marketing have been widely recognized and celebrated. His work has earned him numerous awards and honors, cementing his status as one of the most influential figures in the field. Some of the notable recognitions include:

1. American Marketing Association (AMA) Distinguished Marketing Educator Award

In 1978, Kotler received the AMA Distinguished Marketing Educator Award, one of the highest honors in the field of marketing education. This award recognized his exceptional contributions to marketing theory and education, as well as his impact on the development of marketing as an academic discipline.

2. Marketing Hall of Fame Induction

Kotler was inducted into the Marketing Hall of Fame in 1978, further acknowledging his significant influence on the field. The Marketing Hall of Fame honors individuals who have made outstanding contributions to marketing, and Kotler's inclusion is a testament to his enduring impact.

3. Paul D. Converse Award

In 1975, Kotler was awarded the Paul D. Converse Award by the American Marketing Association. This prestigious award recognizes individuals who have made major contributions to marketing theory and practice. Kotler's innovative ideas and extensive body of work have earned him this distinguished honor.

4. Sheth Foundation Medal for Exceptional Contribution to Marketing Scholarship

In 2017, Kotler received the Sheth Foundation Medal for Exceptional Contribution to Marketing Scholarship. This award celebrates his lifetime achievements and his profound influence on marketing scholarship and practice.

5. Honorary Degrees and Global Recognition

Kotler has been awarded honorary degrees from numerous universities around the world, including the University of Stockholm, University of Zurich, Athens University of Economics and Business, and many others. These honorary degrees reflect his global influence and the widespread recognition of his contributions to marketing.

6. Author of the Century Award

In 2011, Kotler was honored with the "Author of the Century" award by the Sales and Marketing Executives International (SMEI). This award recognized his unparalleled contributions to marketing literature and his role in shaping the modern marketing landscape.

7. Influential Thought Leader

Kotler's influence extends beyond academia and awards. He has been a sought-after speaker and thought leader, delivering keynote addresses at major marketing conferences and events worldwide. His insights and thought leadership have inspired countless marketing professionals and academics to adopt more innovative and strategic approaches to marketing.

Philip Kotler's biography and contributions to marketing theory are a testament to his profound impact on the field. His academic background and early influences provided the foundation for his groundbreaking work, which has shaped modern marketing practices and theories. Through his key publications, including "Marketing Management," the concept of market segmentation, the societal marketing concept, "Marketing 3.0," and his work on nonprofit marketing, Kotler has provided invaluable insights and frameworks that continue to guide marketers today.

Kotler's numerous awards and recognitions reflect the widespread acknowledgment of his contributions and his status as a leading figure in marketing. His influence extends globally, with his theories and principles being taught in business schools around the world and applied by marketing professionals in diverse industries.

As we continue to navigate the complexities of the modern marketing landscape, Kotler's legacy serves as a guiding light, reminding us of the importance of customer-centricity, strategic thinking, and ethical considerations in marketing. His work has not only advanced the field of marketing but has also inspired generations of marketers to pursue excellence and innovation in their practice.

The Evolution of Marketing from Kotler's Perspective

Philip Kotler, often referred to as the "Father of Modern Marketing," has profoundly influenced how we understand and practice marketing. His perspective on the evolution of marketing reflects the transition from a product-centric approach to a more customer-centric one, the significant role of technology and globalization, and his vision for the future of marketing. This section explores these aspects in detail, followed by an analysis of consumer behavior and market segmentation.

From Product-Centric to Customer-Centric

In the early stages of marketing, businesses primarily focused on the products they created. This product-centric approach emphasized the features and benefits of the products, with the assumption that superior products would naturally attract customers. However, Philip Kotler's work highlighted the limitations of this perspective and championed a shift towards a customer-centric approach.

Product-Centric Marketing

Product-centric marketing, which dominated much of the early 20th century, revolved around the idea that the key to business success lay in producing high-quality products. Companies invested heavily in research and development to create innovative products, believing that these would meet consumer needs and generate sales. Advertising campaigns during this period often focused on showcasing the technical specifications and unique features of the products.

While this approach yielded some success, it often led to a disconnect between what companies produced and what customers actually wanted. Businesses were more focused on their products than on understanding the needs and preferences of their target market.

The Shift to Customer-Centric Marketing

Kotler's revolutionary idea was that businesses should shift their focus from the products themselves to the customers who buy them. This customer-centric approach emphasizes understanding and meeting the needs and wants of customers. Kotler argued that businesses should view their products through the lens of customer benefits rather than technical features.

This shift required a fundamental change in how companies operated. Instead of asking, "What can we produce?" companies began to ask, "What do our customers need and want?" This customer-centric approach involves extensive market research to gather insights into consumer preferences, behaviors, and pain points. By understanding their customers better, companies can create products and services that genuinely meet their needs, leading to higher customer satisfaction and loyalty.

Kotler's customer-centric philosophy is encapsulated in his concept of the marketing mix, or the 4 Ps: Product, Price, Place, and Promotion. He emphasized that these elements should be designed with the customer in mind, ensuring that every aspect of the marketing strategy aligns with customer needs and preferences.

Benefits of Customer-Centric Marketing

The transition to customer-centric marketing has several significant benefits:

- Increased Customer Satisfaction: By focusing on customer needs and preferences, businesses can create products and services that provide real value, leading to higher customer satisfaction.

- Improved Customer Loyalty: Satisfied customers are more likely to remain loyal to a brand and make repeat purchases, which is crucial for long-term business success.

- Better Market Differentiation: Understanding and meeting customer needs allows businesses to differentiate themselves from competitors by offering unique value propositions.

- Enhanced Brand Reputation: Companies that prioritize customer satisfaction often enjoy a stronger brand reputation, as customers appreciate businesses that genuinely care about their needs.

The Role of Technology and Globalization

Kotler has also highlighted the profound impact of technology and globalization on marketing practices. These forces have transformed the way businesses operate and interact with their customers, creating both opportunities and challenges.

Impact of Technology

Technology has revolutionized marketing in several key ways:

- Digital Marketing: The rise of the internet and digital technologies has given birth to digital marketing, which includes online advertising, social media marketing, email marketing, and more. These platforms allow businesses to reach a global audience and engage with customers in real-time.

- Data Analytics: Advances in data analytics have enabled businesses to collect and analyze vast amounts of data about consumer behavior. This data-driven approach allows for more targeted and personalized marketing strategies, improving effectiveness and ROI.

- Automation and AI: Marketing automation tools and artificial intelligence (AI) have streamlined many marketing processes, from email campaigns to customer service. AI-powered tools can analyze consumer data, predict trends, and personalize marketing messages at scale.

- E-commerce: Technology has also transformed the way products are bought and sold. E-commerce platforms allow businesses to reach customers globally, providing a convenient and efficient shopping experience.

Impact of Globalization

Globalization has expanded the reach of businesses, allowing them to operate in multiple markets around the world. This global perspective has significant implications for marketing:

- Cultural Sensitivity: Marketing strategies must be adapted to suit different cultural contexts. What works in one country may not be effective in another, so businesses must understand and respect cultural differences.

- Global Competition: Globalization has increased competition, as businesses now compete with companies from around the world. This has driven innovation and pushed companies to improve their products and marketing strategies.

- Cross-Border Collaboration: Globalization has facilitated collaboration between companies from different countries, leading to new partnerships and opportunities for growth.

Challenges and Opportunities

While technology and globalization offer numerous opportunities, they also present challenges. Businesses must navigate issues such as data privacy, cybersecurity, and regulatory compliance in different markets. However, those that can effectively leverage technology and adapt to a globalized world can achieve significant competitive advantages.
The Future of Marketing

Philip Kotler's insights into the future of marketing emphasize the importance of adaptability, innovation, and a continued focus on the customer. Here are some key trends and predictions for the future of marketing:

1. Personalization

The demand for personalized experiences will continue to grow. Advances in AI and data analytics will enable businesses to deliver highly personalized marketing messages and offers based on individual consumer preferences and behaviors. Personalization will become a key differentiator in a crowded marketplace.

2. Ethical and Sustainable Marketing

Consumers are increasingly concerned about social and environmental issues. Businesses will need to adopt more ethical and sustainable marketing practices, focusing on transparency, corporate social responsibility (CSR), and sustainability. Brands that demonstrate a commitment to these values will build stronger relationships with their customers.

3. Customer Experience

Customer experience (CX) will become a critical focus for businesses. Companies will invest in creating seamless, enjoyable experiences across all touchpoints, from online interactions to in-store visits. A positive customer experience will be essential for driving customer loyalty and advocacy.

4. Integration of Technology

Emerging technologies such as virtual reality (VR), augmented reality (AR), and the Internet of Things

(IoT) will play a significant role in marketing. These technologies will enable immersive and interactive experiences, allowing businesses to engage with customers in new and exciting ways.

5. Data Privacy and Security

As businesses collect more data about their customers, data privacy and security will become paramount. Companies will need to implement robust data protection measures and comply with regulations such as the General Data Protection Regulation (GDPR). Building trust with customers through responsible data practices will be crucial.

6. Global Collaboration

Globalization will continue to shape marketing strategies. Businesses will need to collaborate across borders, leveraging global talent and resources to create innovative marketing campaigns. Understanding and respecting cultural differences will be essential for success in diverse markets. Understanding Consumer Behavior and Market Segmentation

Understanding consumer behavior and effectively segmenting the market are critical components of modern marketing. Philip Kotler's work has provided valuable insights into these areas, helping businesses develop more targeted and effective marketing strategies.

Analyzing Consumer Needs and Wants

To effectively meet the needs and wants of consumers, businesses must first understand what drives their behavior. Kotler's framework for analyzing consumer behavior involves several key components:

1. Psychological Factors

Psychological factors play a significant role in shaping consumer behavior. These include:

- Motivation: Understanding what motivates consumers to make a purchase is crucial. Motivations can be driven by basic needs (e.g., food, shelter) or higher-level desires (e.g., status, self-fulfillment).

- Perception: How consumers perceive a product or brand can influence their purchasing decisions. Marketers must understand how their messages are perceived and how to shape perceptions in a positive way.

- Learning: Past experiences influence future behavior. Consumers learn from their experiences with products and brands, which affects their future choices.

- Beliefs and Attitudes: Consumers' beliefs and attitudes toward a product or brand can impact their purchasing decisions. Marketers need to understand and influence these beliefs and attitudes.

2. Social Factors

Social factors also play a critical role in consumer behavior. These include:

- Reference Groups: The groups to which consumers belong or aspire to belong (e.g., family, friends, social networks) can influence their behavior. Consumers often look to these groups for guidance and validation.

- Family: Family members can significantly influence purchasing decisions, particularly for products used within the household.

- Social Roles and Status: Consumers' roles and status within their social networks can affect their buying behavior. For example, a person's job or social position may influence the types of products they purchase.

3. Cultural Factors

Cultural factors encompass the broader societal influences on consumer behavior. These include:

- Culture: The shared values, beliefs, and customs of a society shape consumer behavior. Marketers must understand the cultural context in which they operate and tailor their strategies accordingly.

- Subculture: Within a larger culture, there may be subcultures with distinct values and behaviors. Identifying and targeting these subcultures can lead to more effective marketing.

- Social Class: Social class can influence consumer preferences and purchasing behavior. Different social classes may have different priorities and spending habits.

4. Personal Factors

Personal factors are individual characteristics that affect consumer behavior. These include:

- Age and Life Cycle Stage: Consumers' needs and preferences change as they age and move through different life stages. Marketers must consider these changes when developing their strategies.

- Occupation: A person's occupation can influence their buying behavior. For example, a business executive may have different needs and preferences than a student.

- Economic Situation: Consumers' financial situations affect their purchasing power and choices. Marketers must consider the economic context in which their target audience operates.

- Lifestyle: Lifestyle reflects consumers' interests, activities, and opinions. Understanding consumers' lifestyles can help marketers develop more targeted and relevant campaigns.

- Personality and Self-Concept: Personality traits

and self-concept influence how consumers perceive and interact with products and brands. Marketers can tailor their messages to resonate with different personality types.
By analyzing these factors, businesses can gain a deeper understanding of consumer behavior and develop marketing strategies that effectively meet the needs and wants of their target audience.

Segmenting the Market

Market segmentation is the process of dividing a broad market into smaller, more defined segments based on shared characteristics. Kotler's work on market segmentation has provided a framework for identifying and targeting these segments effectively.

1. Demographic Segmentation

Demographic segmentation involves dividing the market based on demographic variables such as age, gender, income, education, and occupation. This type of segmentation is widely used because demographic data is relatively easy to obtain and analyze.

For example, a company selling luxury watches may target high-income individuals, while a brand offering budget-friendly products may focus on middle-income households. Demographic segmentation helps businesses tailor their marketing messages to the specific needs and preferences of different demographic groups.

2. Geographic Segmentation

Geographic segmentation divides the market based on

geographic factors such as location, climate, and population density. This approach is useful for businesses that operate in multiple regions and need to tailor their strategies to local conditions.

For instance, a clothing brand may offer different products and marketing campaigns in tropical regions compared to colder climates. Geographic segmentation allows businesses to address the unique needs and preferences of consumers in different locations.

3. Psychographic Segmentation

Psychographic segmentation goes beyond demographics and focuses on consumers' lifestyles, interests, values, and personalities. This approach provides deeper insights into consumer behavior and allows for more personalized marketing strategies.

For example, a fitness brand may target health-conscious individuals who value an active lifestyle, while a luxury brand may focus on consumers who prioritize status and exclusivity. Psychographic segmentation helps businesses create more relevant and engaging marketing messages.

4. Behavioral Segmentation

Behavioral segmentation divides the market based on consumers' behavior, such as their purchasing habits, usage patterns, and brand loyalty. This approach allows businesses to target consumers based on their interactions with the brand.

For instance, a company may identify a segment of

frequent buyers who make repeat purchases and target them with loyalty programs and personalized offers. Behavioral segmentation helps businesses understand and address the specific behaviors and needs of different consumer groups.

5. Benefit Segmentation

Benefit segmentation focuses on the specific benefits that consumers seek from a product or service. This approach identifies segments based on the value that consumers derive from the product.

For example, a skincare brand may segment its market based on consumers seeking anti-aging benefits, acne treatment, or hydration. By understanding the specific benefits that different segments seek, businesses can tailor their marketing messages to highlight those benefits.
Targeting and Positioning Strategies

Once the market has been segmented, businesses must decide which segments to target and how to position their products or services to meet the needs of those segments. Kotler's work provides valuable insights into targeting and positioning strategies.

1. Targeting Strategies

Targeting involves selecting one or more market segments to focus on. There are several targeting strategies that businesses can adopt:

- Undifferentiated Marketing: Also known as mass marketing, this strategy involves

targeting the entire market with a single marketing mix. This approach is useful for products with broad appeal and limited differentiation.
- Differentiated Marketing: This strategy involves targeting multiple segments with different marketing mixes for each segment. This approach allows businesses to address the specific needs of each segment and create more tailored marketing messages.

- Concentrated Marketing: Also known as niche marketing, this strategy involves focusing on a single segment with a specialized marketing mix. This approach is useful for businesses with limited resources or those serving a specific niche market.

- Micromarketing: This strategy involves targeting individual consumers or very small segments with highly personalized marketing messages. Advances in technology and data analytics have made micromarketing more feasible and effective.

2. Positioning Strategies

Positioning involves creating a distinct image and identity for a product or brand in the minds of consumers. Effective positioning differentiates the product from competitors and highlights its unique value proposition. Kotler's framework for positioning includes several key steps:

- Identify Competitive Advantages: Determine

the unique features and benefits that set the product apart from competitors. These advantages could be based on product attributes, quality, price, or customer service.
- Choose a Positioning Strategy: Select a positioning strategy that aligns with the target segment's needs and preferences. Common positioning strategies include positioning based on product attributes, benefits, usage occasions, or customer segments.

- Communicate the Positioning: Develop a clear and compelling message that communicates the chosen positioning to the target segment. This message should be consistently reinforced across all marketing channels and touchpoints.

- Evaluate and Adjust: Continuously monitor the effectiveness of the positioning strategy and make adjustments as needed. This involves tracking consumer perceptions, competitive dynamics, and market trends.

Effective targeting and positioning strategies help businesses connect with their target audience, differentiate their products, and create a strong brand identity.

Philip Kotler's perspective on the evolution of marketing highlights the shift from product-centric to customer-centric approaches, the impact of technology and globalization, and the future of marketing. His work has provided valuable insights into understanding consumer behavior and market segmentation, helping businesses develop more targeted and effective marketing strategies.

By analyzing consumer needs and wants, segmenting the market, and implementing effective targeting and positioning strategies, businesses can better meet the needs of their customers and achieve long-term success. Kotler's principles and frameworks continue to guide modern marketers, emphasizing the importance of customer-centricity, strategic thinking, and adaptability in an ever-changing marketing landscape.

The 4 Ps of Marketing (Product, Price, Place, Promotion)

Philip Kotler's framework for the 4 Ps of Marketing—Product, Price, Place, and Promotion—has been foundational in shaping modern marketing practices. Each of these elements plays a critical role in developing an effective marketing strategy. This section explores how businesses can develop the right product, implement pricing strategies, choose distribution channels, and execute promotional tactics.

Developing the Right Product

The product is the core of the marketing mix. It represents the goods or services that a business offers to meet the needs and wants of consumers. Developing the right product involves several key considerations:

1. Understanding Consumer Needs and Preferences

The first step in product development is understanding what consumers need and want. This involves conducting market research to gather insights into consumer behavior, preferences, and pain points. Businesses can use surveys, focus groups, and data analytics to identify trends and patterns that inform product development.

2. Creating Value

A successful product must create value for the consumer. This value can be functional (solving a problem or fulfilling a need), emotional (providing pleasure or satisfaction), or social (enhancing status or identity). The product should offer benefits that resonate with the target audience and differentiate it from competitors.

3. Innovation and Differentiation

Innovation is critical in developing a product that stands out in the market. This can involve introducing new features, improving existing ones, or creating entirely new products. Differentiation is about making the product unique and appealing to consumers. This can be achieved through superior quality, design, functionality, or branding.

4. Product Lifecycle Management

Understanding the product lifecycle—introduction, growth, maturity, and decline—is essential for managing a product's market presence. Each stage requires different strategies for marketing, pricing, and distribution. For example, during the introduction stage, the focus might be on building awareness, while in the maturity stage, the emphasis might shift to differentiation and retention.

5. Branding and Packaging

Branding and packaging play a significant role in shaping consumer perceptions and experiences. A strong brand identity and attractive packaging can enhance the product's appeal and create a lasting impression. Consistent branding helps build trust and loyalty, while effective packaging can convey quality and functionality.

Pricing Strategies

Price is a critical element of the marketing mix that directly impacts a company's revenue and profitability. Pricing strategies should reflect the value of the product, the target market, and competitive dynamics. Key considerations for pricing strategies include:

1. Cost-Based Pricing

Cost-based pricing involves setting prices based on the costs of producing and delivering the product plus a desired profit margin. This approach ensures that all costs are covered and a profit is made. However, it may not always reflect the value perceived by consumers or market conditions.

2. Value-Based Pricing

Value-based pricing sets prices based on the perceived value of the product to the consumer. This approach requires a deep understanding of how consumers value the product's benefits and their willingness to pay. Value-based pricing can lead to higher margins and stronger customer relationships.

3. Competitive Pricing

Competitive pricing involves setting prices based on the prices of competitors' products. This strategy is common in highly competitive markets where price is a key differentiator. Businesses may choose to price their products lower to attract price-sensitive consumers or higher to position their products as premium offerings.

4. Penetration Pricing

Penetration pricing sets a low initial price to quickly gain market share and attract a large number of customers. This strategy is often used for new products entering a competitive market. Once market share is established, prices may be gradually increased.

5. Skimming Pricing

Skimming pricing involves setting a high initial price to target consumers who are willing to pay a premium for a new or innovative product. This strategy can maximize short-term profits and help recoup development costs. Over time, prices may be reduced to attract more price-sensitive segments.

6. Psychological Pricing

Psychological pricing takes into account the psychological impact of pricing on consumers. Techniques such as pricing just below a round number (e.g., $9.99 instead of $10.00) can create the perception of a lower price. Other methods include using prestige pricing for luxury products to enhance perceived value.

Distribution Channels

Place, or distribution, refers to the channels through which a product reaches the consumer. Effective distribution ensures that products are available where and when consumers want them. Key considerations for choosing distribution channels include:

1. Direct Distribution

Direct distribution involves selling products directly to consumers without intermediaries. This can be done through company-owned stores, websites, or direct sales teams. Direct distribution allows businesses to maintain control over the customer experience and capture higher margins.

2. Indirect Distribution

Indirect distribution uses intermediaries such as wholesalers, retailers, or distributors to reach consumers. This approach can expand market reach and reduce the burden of logistics and distribution management. However, it may result in lower margins and less control over the customer experience.

3. Multichannel Distribution

Multichannel distribution combines direct and indirect channels to reach a broader audience. For example, a company might sell its products through its website, physical stores, and third-party retailers. This strategy provides flexibility and convenience for consumers, enhancing overall market coverage.

4. E-commerce and Online Distribution

The rise of e-commerce has transformed distribution strategies. Online distribution allows businesses to reach a global audience and provide a convenient shopping experience. E-commerce platforms, online marketplaces, and direct-to-consumer websites are essential components of modern distribution strategies.

5. Channel Partner Relationships

Building strong relationships with channel partners is crucial for effective distribution. This involves selecting reliable partners, providing training and support, and maintaining open communication. Collaborative relationships can enhance product availability, improve customer service, and drive sales.

6. Logistics and Supply Chain Management

Efficient logistics and supply chain management are critical for ensuring timely and cost-effective distribution. This includes managing inventory levels, optimizing transportation, and coordinating with suppliers and distributors. Technology solutions such as inventory management systems and supply chain analytics can enhance efficiency and responsiveness.

Promotional Tactics

Promotion encompasses the various tactics used to communicate the value of a product to the target audience. Effective promotion involves a mix of advertising, sales promotion, public relations, personal selling, and digital marketing. Key promotional tactics include:

1. Advertising

Advertising is a paid form of promotion that reaches a broad audience through various media channels, including television, radio, print, online, and outdoor. Effective advertising campaigns convey a clear message, create brand awareness, and drive consumer action.

2. Sales Promotion

Sales promotion involves short-term incentives to encourage purchases, such as discounts, coupons, contests, and free samples. These tactics can boost sales, attract new customers, and incentivize repeat purchases.

3. Public Relations

Public relations (PR) focuses on building and maintaining a positive image and reputation for the brand. PR activities include media relations, press releases, events, and sponsorships. Effective PR can enhance brand credibility, generate positive media coverage, and foster goodwill.

4. Personal Selling
Personal selling involves direct interaction between sales representatives and potential customers. This approach is effective for complex or high-value products that require personalized explanations and demonstrations. Personal selling builds relationships and trust, leading to higher conversion rates.

5. Digital Marketing

Digital marketing encompasses various online tactics, including social media marketing, email marketing, content marketing, search engine optimization (SEO), and pay-per-click (PPC) advertising. Digital marketing allows for precise targeting, real-time engagement, and measurable results.

6. Integrated Marketing Communications (IMC)

IMC ensures that all promotional activities are coordinated and consistent across different channels. This holistic approach creates a unified brand message and enhances the overall impact of promotional efforts. IMC involves aligning advertising, sales promotion, PR, personal selling, and digital marketing to achieve synergy.

Applying Kotler's Principles in the Digital Age

Philip Kotler's principles remain highly relevant in the

digital age, where technology and online platforms have transformed the marketing landscape. This section explores how businesses can apply Kotler's principles through digital marketing strategies, e-commerce, and the integration of traditional and digital marketing.

Digital Marketing Strategies

Digital marketing has become a cornerstone of modern marketing practices. Kotler's principles can be effectively applied to digital marketing strategies to enhance their effectiveness and impact.

1. Content Marketing

Content marketing involves creating and distributing valuable, relevant, and consistent content to attract and engage a target audience. Kotler's emphasis on understanding consumer needs and preferences aligns with the principles of content marketing. By providing content that addresses consumers' interests and pain points, businesses can build trust and authority.

Effective content marketing strategies include blog posts, articles, videos, infographics, and e-books. These content formats educate and inform the audience, driving traffic, and generating leads. Additionally, content marketing supports SEO efforts by improving search engine rankings.

2. Social Media Marketing

Social media platforms offer powerful tools for

engaging with consumers and building brand communities. Kotler's principles of customer-centricity and engagement are central to social media marketing. Businesses can use social media to interact with customers, gather feedback, and create personalized experiences.

Successful social media marketing involves creating engaging content, responding to comments and messages, and running targeted ad campaigns. Platforms such as Facebook, Instagram, Twitter, LinkedIn, and TikTok provide diverse opportunities for reaching different audience segments.

3. Email Marketing

Email marketing remains one of the most effective digital marketing channels for nurturing leads and maintaining customer relationships. Kotler's focus on personalized and relevant communication aligns with best practices in email marketing. Businesses can use email to deliver tailored content, product recommendations, and special offers based on customer preferences.

Segmentation and automation are key components of successful email marketing. By segmenting their email lists based on demographics, behaviors, and purchase history, businesses can send more targeted and relevant messages. Automation tools enable timely and consistent communication with subscribers.

4. Search Engine Optimization (SEO)

SEO is the practice of optimizing a website to rank

higher in search engine results pages (SERPs). Kotler's emphasis on providing value and understanding consumer behavior is integral to SEO. By optimizing their websites for relevant keywords and creating high-quality content, businesses can attract organic traffic and improve visibility.

Key SEO strategies include on-page optimization (e.g., meta tags, headers, and keyword usage), off-page optimization (e.g., backlinks and social signals), and technical SEO (e.g., site speed and mobile-friendliness). Continuous monitoring and analysis of SEO performance help businesses adapt their strategies to changing algorithms and trends.

5. Pay-Per-Click (PPC) Advertising

PPC advertising involves placing ads on search engines, social media platforms, and other websites, and paying only when users click on the ads. Kotler's principles of targeted and data-driven marketing are essential for effective PPC campaigns. By targeting specific keywords and demographics, businesses can reach their desired audience with precision.

Successful PPC campaigns require thorough keyword research, compelling ad copy, and optimized landing pages. Tools such as Google Ads and Facebook Ads provide detailed analytics to measure performance and adjust strategies in real-time.

6. Influencer Marketing

Influencer marketing leverages the reach and credibility of influencers to promote products and services. Kotler's principles of building relationships and trust align with the core of influencer marketing. By partnering with influencers who resonate with their target audience, businesses can amplify their message and enhance brand authenticity.

Effective influencer marketing involves identifying relevant influencers, developing authentic collaborations, and measuring the impact of campaigns. Micro-influencers (those with smaller but highly engaged followings) can be particularly effective for niche markets.

E-Commerce and Online Consumer Behavior

E-commerce has revolutionized the way consumers shop and interact with brands. Understanding online consumer behavior and optimizing e-commerce strategies are crucial for success in the digital age.

1. Consumer Journey in E-Commerce

The consumer journey in e-commerce consists of several stages, including awareness, consideration, purchase, and post-purchase. Kotler's principles of understanding consumer behavior and meeting their needs are vital at each stage.

- Awareness: At this stage, consumers become aware of a brand or product through digital marketing efforts such as SEO, social media, and online ads. Creating engaging content and ensuring visibility in search results are key.

- Consideration: During the consideration stage,

consumers evaluate different options. Providing detailed product information, reviews, and comparisons helps consumers make informed decisions.

- Purchase: The purchase stage involves completing the transaction. A seamless and secure checkout process, multiple payment options, and clear return policies enhance the buying experience.

- Post-Purchase: Post-purchase interactions, such as follow-up emails, customer support, and loyalty programs, are essential for retaining customers and encouraging repeat purchases.

2. Personalization in E-Commerce

Personalization is a powerful strategy for enhancing the online shopping experience. By leveraging data on consumer preferences and behaviors, businesses can deliver tailored product recommendations, personalized offers, and relevant content.

Personalization tools use algorithms and machine learning to analyze data and create individualized experiences. For example, e-commerce platforms can display personalized product recommendations based on a customer's browsing and purchase history.

3. Mobile Commerce

Mobile commerce (m-commerce) has become increasingly important as more consumers use smartphones and tablets for online shopping. Optimizing the mobile shopping experience is crucial for capturing this growing segment.

Key strategies for m-commerce include responsive website design, mobile-friendly navigation, fast loading times, and simplified checkout processes. Mobile apps can also enhance the shopping experience by providing additional features such as push notifications and in-app purchases.

4. Social Commerce

Social commerce integrates e-commerce with social media platforms, allowing consumers to discover and purchase products directly through social media. This approach leverages the social aspect of shopping and the influence of social networks.

Platforms like Instagram and Facebook have introduced shopping features that enable businesses to showcase products and facilitate purchases within the app. Social commerce strategies include creating shoppable posts, using influencer collaborations, and running targeted ad campaigns.

5. Customer Reviews and UGC

Customer reviews and user-generated content (UGC) play a significant role in e-commerce. Reviews provide social proof and influence purchasing decisions, while UGC such as photos and videos enhances brand authenticity.

Encouraging customers to leave reviews and share

their experiences helps build trust and credibility. Highlighting positive reviews and UGC on product pages and social media can drive engagement and conversions.

6. Analytics and Optimization

Data analytics is essential for understanding online consumer behavior and optimizing e-commerce strategies. By tracking key metrics such as traffic, conversion rates, average order value, and customer lifetime value, businesses can identify areas for improvement and refine their approaches.

A/B testing is a valuable tool for optimizing various elements of the e-commerce experience, from website design to marketing campaigns. Continuous monitoring and analysis ensure that strategies remain effective and aligned with consumer preferences.
Integrating Traditional and Digital Marketing

While digital marketing has become a dominant force, traditional marketing channels still play a vital role in a comprehensive marketing strategy. Integrating traditional and digital marketing allows businesses to reach a broader audience and create cohesive campaigns.

1. Consistent Branding

Maintaining consistent branding across traditional and digital channels is essential for creating a unified brand identity. This involves using the same logos, colors, messaging, and tone of voice across all touchpoints.

Consistent branding reinforces brand recognition and trust, ensuring that consumers have a seamless experience regardless of the channel. Integrated marketing communications (IMC) help align all promotional efforts and create a cohesive brand narrative.

2. Cross-Channel Campaigns

Cross-channel campaigns leverage both traditional and digital media to maximize reach and impact. For example, a product launch might include TV commercials, print ads, social media promotions, and email marketing.

By coordinating efforts across multiple channels, businesses can create synergistic effects that amplify their message. Cross-channel campaigns also provide multiple touchpoints for engaging with the audience and driving conversions.

3. Leveraging Data and Insights

Data collected from digital marketing efforts can inform traditional marketing strategies and vice versa. For example, insights from social media analytics can help refine print ad copy, while data from in-store purchases can inform online marketing campaigns.

Integrating data from various sources provides a comprehensive view of consumer behavior and preferences. This holistic approach enables businesses to make more informed decisions and optimize their marketing strategies.

4. Combining Offline and Online Experiences

Creating seamless offline and online experiences enhances customer satisfaction and engagement. For example, businesses can offer in-store pickup for online orders, use QR codes in print ads to drive traffic to their website, or provide digital coupons that can be redeemed in physical stores.

Combining offline and online experiences meets consumers' expectations for convenience and flexibility. It also allows businesses to leverage the strengths of each channel to create a more comprehensive customer journey.

5. Event Marketing and Digital Integration

Event marketing, such as trade shows, conferences, and product launches, can be enhanced through digital integration. Live streaming events, using social media to promote and engage attendees, and collecting leads through online registration forms are effective strategies.

Digital tools can extend the reach and impact of events, allowing businesses to engage with a wider audience and create lasting impressions. Event-specific hashtags, live updates, and post-event follow-ups keep the audience engaged and connected.

6. Measuring and Evaluating Performance

Measuring the performance of integrated marketing campaigns involves tracking key metrics across traditional and digital channels. This includes analyzing ROI, engagement, reach, and conversion rates.

Using analytics tools and marketing dashboards, businesses can monitor the effectiveness of their campaigns and identify areas for improvement. Continuous evaluation and optimization ensure that integrated marketing efforts remain aligned with business goals and deliver desired outcomes.

Philip Kotler's principles of the 4 Ps of Marketing—Product, Price, Place, and Promotion—remain foundational in both traditional and digital marketing contexts. Developing the right product, implementing effective pricing strategies, choosing appropriate distribution channels, and executing compelling promotional tactics are essential for marketing success.

In the digital age, Kotler's principles can be applied through digital marketing strategies, e-commerce optimization, and the integration of traditional and digital marketing. By understanding consumer behavior, leveraging data and technology, and maintaining consistent branding, businesses can create impactful marketing campaigns that resonate with their target audience.

Kotler's insights continue to guide marketers in navigating the complexities of the modern marketing landscape, emphasizing the importance of customer-centricity, strategic thinking, and adaptability. As technology and consumer preferences evolve, Kotler's principles provide a timeless framework for achieving marketing excellence and driving business growth.

Chapter 4:

Mary Kay Ash Empowerment and Direct Sales

Mary Kay Ash was a visionary entrepreneur whose innovative approach to direct sales and commitment to empowering women transformed the cosmetics industry. Her life story is a testament to the power of determination, creativity, and a passion for helping others succeed. This section explores Mary Kay Ash's early life and career path, the inspiration behind Mary Kay Cosmetics, and the remarkable journey of building her business.

Early Life and Career Path

Mary Kay Ash was born Mary Kathlyn Wagner on May 12, 1918, in Hot Wells, Texas. Her early life was marked by hardship and responsibility. Her father was chronically ill, which required her mother to work long hours to support the family. As a result, Mary Kay assumed significant responsibilities at a young age, managing the household and caring for her father and siblings.

Despite these challenges, Mary Kay excelled in school and exhibited a strong work ethic. After graduating from high school, she attended the University of

Houston briefly before her family's financial situation forced her to leave and seek employment. Her early jobs included selling books door-to-door, a role that would later influence her approach to sales and entrepreneurship.

In 1939, Mary Kay married Ben Rogers, and they had three children. However, her marriage ended in divorce in 1952, leaving her to support her children as a single mother. Determined to succeed, she embarked on a career in direct sales, joining Stanley Home Products. Her talent for sales quickly became evident, and she earned numerous awards and accolades for her performance.

Mary Kay's early career in direct sales laid the foundation for her future success. She learned the importance of building relationships, understanding customer needs, and providing exceptional service. These experiences would later shape her vision for Mary Kay Cosmetics.

The Inspiration Behind Mary Kay Cosmetics

Mary Kay Ash's journey to founding her own company was driven by a combination of personal experiences and professional frustrations. After spending more than two decades in direct sales, she faced a pivotal moment in her career that would ultimately lead to the creation of Mary Kay Cosmetics.

Professional Frustrations and Gender Discrimination

Despite her outstanding performance and

contributions to the companies she worked for, Mary Kay repeatedly encountered gender discrimination. She was often passed over for promotions in favor of less qualified men, a common practice at the time. These experiences left her feeling undervalued and frustrated, but they also fueled her determination to create a different kind of business environment.

A Dream Realized

In 1963, at the age of 45, Mary Kay decided to retire from her job and write a book to help women in business. As she began writing, she realized that she had the blueprint for a business that could empower women and provide them with opportunities that she had been denied. This realization sparked the idea for Mary Kay Cosmetics.

Mary Kay envisioned a company that would offer high-quality beauty products while providing women with the chance to achieve financial independence and personal growth. Her goal was to create an environment where women could succeed based on their abilities and hard work, without facing the barriers and biases she had experienced.

Building the Business

With a clear vision and a $5,000 investment from her savings, Mary Kay embarked on the journey to build her business. She was joined by her 20-year-old son, Richard Rogers, who would play a crucial role in the company's operations and growth.

Product Development and Initial Challenges

Mary Kay's first step was to develop a line of beauty products that she believed in. She purchased a skin care formula from a local tanner who had been using it to keep his hands soft. Recognizing its potential, she refined the formula and created her initial product line, which included skin care products and cosmetics.

The early days were challenging. Mary Kay and Richard faced skepticism and financial constraints. They operated out of a small storefront in Dallas, Texas, and relied heavily on personal relationships and word-of-mouth marketing. Despite these obstacles, Mary Kay's unwavering belief in her vision and her determination to succeed kept her going.

The Beauty Consultant Model

One of Mary Kay's most innovative ideas was the creation of the "Beauty Consultant" model. Instead of relying on traditional retail channels, she developed a direct sales model that empowered women to become independent beauty consultants. These consultants would sell Mary Kay products directly to customers, offering personalized service and beauty advice.

The beauty consultant model was designed to provide women with flexible work opportunities and the potential for financial independence. Mary Kay believed that women could achieve success on their terms, balancing their careers with their personal lives. This approach resonated with many women, especially those looking for opportunities to earn income while managing family responsibilities.

Empowerment and Recognition

Mary Kay's commitment to empowering women extended beyond providing business opportunities. She created a supportive and motivational environment that celebrated achievements and fostered personal growth. The company's culture was built on the principles of recognition, encouragement, and positivity.

Mary Kay implemented a system of incentives and rewards to recognize the achievements of her beauty consultants. These incentives included everything from diamond rings and luxury vacations to the iconic pink Cadillac, which became a symbol of success within the Mary Kay community. This emphasis on recognition and celebration helped build a strong sense of loyalty and motivation among the consultants.

Expansion and Growth

Mary Kay Cosmetics quickly gained traction, thanks to the quality of its products and the dedication of its beauty consultants. The company's innovative approach to direct sales, combined with Mary Kay's leadership and vision, propelled it to success.

By the end of its first year, Mary Kay Cosmetics had generated over $198,000 in sales. The company continued to grow rapidly, expanding its product line and reaching new markets. Mary Kay's leadership style, characterized by her hands-on involvement and genuine care for her consultants, played a significant role in the company's expansion.

International Expansion

Mary Kay's vision extended beyond the United States. In the late 1970s, the company began its international expansion, entering markets such as Canada, Australia, and Mexico. Mary Kay's commitment to empowering women transcended cultural boundaries, and the company's principles resonated with women around the world.

Today, Mary Kay Cosmetics operates in more than 40 countries, with millions of beauty consultants continuing the legacy of empowerment and direct sales that Mary Kay Ash established.

Philanthropy and Legacy

Mary Kay Ash's impact extended beyond the business world. She was a philanthropist who believed in giving back to the community. In 1996, she founded the Mary Kay Ash Charitable Foundation, which supports causes related to cancer research and domestic violence prevention. The foundation reflects her commitment to making a positive difference in the lives of women and their families.

Mary Kay Ash passed away on November 22, 2001, but her legacy lives on through the company she founded and the millions of lives she touched. Her innovative approach to direct sales, her dedication to empowering women, and her unwavering belief in the potential of individuals continue to inspire entrepreneurs and business leaders worldwide.

Mary Kay Ash's journey from a determined young woman facing gender discrimination to a visionary entrepreneur who transformed the cosmetics industry is a story of resilience, innovation, and empowerment. Through the founding of Mary Kay Cosmetics, she created a business model that not only provided high-quality beauty products but also offered women opportunities for financial independence and personal growth.

Mary Kay's commitment to empowering women, her innovative beauty consultant model, and her emphasis on recognition and support created a unique and enduring business culture. Her legacy extends beyond the success of her company, as she continues to inspire generations of entrepreneurs to pursue their dreams and make a positive impact in the world.

Mary Kay Ash's life and work remind us that with vision, determination, and a commitment to helping others, we can overcome obstacles and achieve greatness. Her story is a powerful testament to the transformative power of empowerment and direct sales, and it serves as a beacon of inspiration for all who seek to make a difference in the world.

The Philosophy of Empowering Women Through Sales

Mary Kay Ash's philosophy of empowering women through sales was a groundbreaking approach that not only revolutionized the cosmetics industry but also provided countless women with opportunities for financial independence and personal growth. This section explores her strategies for creating opportunities for women, the importance of recognition and rewards, and how she built a supportive culture within Mary Kay Cosmetics.

Creating Opportunities for Women

Mary Kay Ash believed in the untapped potential of women and was determined to create a business model that allowed women to succeed on their terms. At a time when career opportunities for women were limited, she envisioned a company that offered flexible work arrangements, financial independence, and personal empowerment.

Flexible Work Arrangements

One of the key aspects of Mary Kay Cosmetics was its flexible work model. Women could become beauty consultants and work from home, set their own hours, and manage their businesses according to their personal schedules. This flexibility was particularly appealing to women who needed to balance work with family responsibilities. It allowed them to earn an income without sacrificing their roles as caregivers and homemakers.

Entrepreneurial Opportunities

Mary Kay Cosmetics offered women the chance to become entrepreneurs. As beauty consultants, they could build their businesses, recruit and train their own teams, and grow their income based on their efforts and achievements. This entrepreneurial model empowered women to take control of their financial futures and develop valuable business skills.

Training and Development

Mary Kay Ash recognized that many women lacked formal business training, so she made education and development a cornerstone of her company. Mary Kay Cosmetics provided comprehensive training programs that covered product knowledge, sales techniques, customer service, and business management. These programs equipped beauty consultants with the skills and confidence needed to succeed.

Supportive Community

Mary Kay Cosmetics fostered a sense of community and support among its beauty consultants. Mary Kay Ash believed in the power of women supporting women, and she encouraged consultants to collaborate, share best practices, and mentor each other. This supportive network helped women build strong relationships, gain valuable insights, and find encouragement in their journeys.

The Importance of Recognition and Rewards

Recognition and rewards were integral to Mary Kay Ash's philosophy. She understood that acknowledging and celebrating achievements motivated individuals and fostered a sense of pride and loyalty. Mary Kay Cosmetics became renowned for its innovative and generous recognition programs.

Recognition Programs

Mary Kay Ash believed that recognition should be public and meaningful. The company implemented various recognition programs to celebrate the accomplishments of its beauty consultants. These programs included awards, ceremonies, and public acknowledgment of achievements. Consultants who reached sales milestones, recruited new team members, or demonstrated exceptional leadership were honored and celebrated.

Incentives and Rewards

In addition to recognition, Mary Kay Cosmetics offered a range of incentives and rewards to motivate consultants. These incentives included luxury items, travel opportunities, and the iconic pink Cadillac, which became a symbol of success within the company. The pink Cadillac, awarded to top-performing consultants, was a visible and aspirational reward that inspired many to strive for excellence.

Empowerment through Achievement

Mary Kay Ash believed that recognition and rewards empowered women by validating their efforts and achievements. By publicly acknowledging their successes, she helped women build self-esteem and confidence. This empowerment extended beyond financial rewards, as it reinforced the idea that women could achieve greatness and make significant contributions to their families and communities.

Creating a Culture of Celebration

The emphasis on recognition and rewards created a culture of celebration within Mary Kay Cosmetics. Achievements were not only celebrated by the individuals who earned them but by the entire community. This culture of celebration fostered camaraderie, motivation, and a positive environment where women felt valued and appreciated.

Building a Supportive Culture

Mary Kay Ash's commitment to building a supportive culture was a key factor in the success of Mary Kay Cosmetics. She believed that a positive and nurturing environment was essential for personal and professional growth. This supportive culture was characterized by encouragement, mentorship, and a sense of belonging.

Encouragement and Positivity

Mary Kay Ash was known for her positive and encouraging leadership style. She believed in focusing on strengths rather than weaknesses and always looked for ways to uplift and inspire others. This positive approach created an environment where consultants felt motivated to pursue their goals and overcome challenges.

Mentorship and Training

Mentorship was a cornerstone of the Mary Kay culture. Experienced beauty consultants and leaders were encouraged to mentor and support newer consultants. This mentorship provided guidance, shared knowledge, and offered a support system that helped consultants navigate their careers. Mary Kay Ash herself was a mentor to many, leading by example and sharing her wisdom and experiences.

Inclusivity and Diversity

Mary Kay Cosmetics embraced inclusivity and diversity, welcoming women from all backgrounds and walks of life. This inclusive approach created a diverse community where different perspectives were valued and celebrated. The company's commitment to diversity was reflected in its product offerings, marketing materials, and corporate policies.

Community and Camaraderie

The sense of community and camaraderie within Mary Kay Cosmetics was a defining feature of its culture. Beauty consultants formed strong bonds and supported each other both personally and professionally. Regular events, conferences, and meetings provided opportunities for consultants to connect, share experiences, and celebrate achievements together.

Empowerment through Support

The supportive culture of Mary Kay Cosmetics empowered women by providing them with the resources, encouragement, and community they needed to succeed. Consultants felt a sense of belonging and purpose, knowing that they were part of a larger mission to empower women and make a positive impact.

The Importance of Personal Connections in Marketing

Mary Kay Ash's success was built on the foundation of personal connections. She understood the value of building strong relationships with customers and how these connections could drive customer loyalty, retention, and word-of-mouth marketing. This section explores relationship-building strategies, customer loyalty and retention, and the power of word-of-mouth in marketing.

Relationship-Building Strategies

Building personal connections with customers is essential for creating lasting relationships and driving business success. Mary Kay Ash's approach to relationship-building involved genuine care, personalized service, and consistent communication.

Genuine Care and Empathy

Mary Kay Ash believed that genuine care and empathy were the cornerstones of successful relationship-building. She encouraged beauty consultants to listen to their customers, understand their needs, and provide solutions that genuinely addressed their concerns. This empathetic approach helped build trust and rapport with customers.

Personalized Service

Providing personalized service was a hallmark of the Mary Kay experience. Beauty consultants offered one-on-one consultations, tailored product recommendations, and personalized beauty advice. By customizing their service to meet the unique needs of each customer, consultants created a more meaningful and memorable experience.

Consistent Communication

Consistent communication was key to maintaining strong relationships with customers. Mary Kay consultants regularly followed up with their customers, providing updates on new products, promotions, and beauty tips. This ongoing communication kept customers engaged and informed, reinforcing their connection to the brand.

Customer Appreciation

Mary Kay Ash understood the importance of showing appreciation to customers. Consultants were encouraged to express gratitude through thank-you notes, small gifts, and special offers. These gestures of appreciation made customers feel valued and strengthened their loyalty to the brand.

Building Trust and Credibility

Trust and credibility were essential components of relationship-building. Mary Kay consultants were trained to provide honest and transparent information about products and services. By being trustworthy and reliable, consultants earned the confidence and loyalty of their customers.

Customer Loyalty and Retention

Customer loyalty and retention are critical for long-term business success. Loyal customers are more likely to make repeat purchases, refer others, and become brand advocates. Mary Kay Ash's strategies for fostering customer loyalty and retention included delivering exceptional service, creating a sense of community, and rewarding loyalty.

Delivering Exceptional Service

Providing exceptional service was a core value of Mary Kay Cosmetics. Consultants were trained to exceed customer expectations by offering high-quality products, personalized attention, and outstanding customer service. Exceptional service created positive experiences that encouraged customers to return.

Creating a Sense of Community

Mary Kay Ash believed in creating a sense of community among customers. Consultants often organized events, workshops, and parties where customers could gather, learn about beauty tips, and try new products. These events fostered a sense of belonging and connection, strengthening customer loyalty.

Rewarding Loyalty

Mary Kay Cosmetics implemented loyalty programs to reward repeat customers. These programs included special discounts, exclusive offers, and early access to new products. By recognizing and rewarding loyal customers, the company encouraged continued engagement and repeat purchases.

Providing Consistent Value

Consistency in delivering value was key to retaining customers. Mary Kay Ash emphasized the importance of maintaining high standards in product quality and customer service. Consistent value ensured that customers remained satisfied and loyal to the brand.

Building Long-Term Relationships

Building long-term relationships with customers was a priority for Mary Kay consultants. Instead of focusing solely on short-term sales, consultants aimed to develop lasting connections with their customers. This long-term approach fostered trust, loyalty, and mutual respect.

The Power of Word-of-Mouth

Word-of-mouth marketing is one of the most powerful and cost-effective forms of promotion. Mary Kay Ash recognized the potential of word-of-mouth to drive business growth and encouraged her consultants to leverage their personal networks to spread the word about Mary Kay products and opportunities.

Leveraging Personal Networks

Mary Kay consultants were encouraged to leverage their personal networks to build their businesses. This involved reaching out to friends, family, neighbors, and acquaintances to introduce them to Mary Kay products and the business opportunity. Personal referrals from trusted sources carried significant weight and credibility.

Creating Memorable Experiences

Creating memorable and positive experiences for customers was key to generating word-of-mouth. When customers had exceptional experiences with Mary Kay products and consultants, they were more likely to share their experiences with others. Satisfied customers became enthusiastic advocates for the brand.

Encouraging Referrals

Mary Kay Cosmetics implemented referral programs to incentivize customers to refer new clients. Consultants offered discounts, gifts, or other rewards to customers who referred their friends and family. These referral programs helped expand the customer base and drive new business.

Utilizing Testimonials and Reviews

Customer testimonials and reviews were powerful tools for word-of-mouth marketing. Mary Kay consultants collected and shared positive feedback from satisfied customers, both online and offline. Testimonials and reviews provided social proof and reinforced the brand's credibility.

Building a Community of Advocates

Mary Kay Ash believed in building a community of advocates who were passionate about the brand. Consultants and customers who believed in the mission and values of Mary Kay Cosmetics became loyal supporters and actively promoted the brand within their networks. This community of advocates played a crucial role in driving word-of-mouth and expanding the reach of the brand.

Mary Kay Ash's philosophy of empowering women through sales, her emphasis on recognition and rewards, and her commitment to building a supportive culture have left an enduring legacy in the business world. Her innovative approach to direct sales provided women with opportunities for financial independence and personal growth, transforming the lives of countless individuals.

Mary Kay's understanding of the importance of personal connections in marketing further contributed to her success. By focusing on relationship-building, customer loyalty and retention, and leveraging the power of word-of-mouth, Mary Kay Cosmetics became a trusted and beloved brand.

Mary Kay Ash's life and work continue to inspire entrepreneurs and business leaders worldwide. Her philosophy of empowerment, her dedication to recognizing and celebrating achievements, and her commitment to creating a positive and supportive culture serve as guiding principles for building successful and impactful businesses. Mary Kay Ash's legacy is a testament to the transformative power of empowerment, recognition, and personal connections in achieving business excellence and making a positive difference in the world.

Strategies for Building a Loyal Salesforce and Customer Base

Mary Kay Ash's success in creating a loyal salesforce and customer base was rooted in her comprehensive strategies for recruitment and training, motivational techniques, and a commitment to customer service excellence. This section delves into these strategies, examining how they contributed to the enduring success of Mary Kay Cosmetics.

Recruitment and Training

Recruitment and training are foundational elements in building a loyal and effective salesforce. Mary Kay Ash's innovative approaches in these areas have become benchmarks for direct sales businesses.

1. Attracting the Right Talent

Mary Kay Ash understood that the success of her company depended on recruiting individuals who were passionate, motivated, and aligned with the company's values. To attract the right talent, Mary Kay Cosmetics emphasized the benefits of becoming a beauty consultant, including the potential for financial independence, flexible working hours, and the opportunity for personal and professional growth.

Recruitment efforts were often conducted through word-of-mouth, leveraging the personal networks of existing consultants. This approach ensured that new recruits were often referred by trusted sources, increasing the likelihood of attracting committed and reliable individuals.

2. Comprehensive Training Programs

Training was a cornerstone of Mary Kay's strategy for building a successful salesforce. Recognizing that many new recruits had little to no sales experience, Mary Kay Cosmetics developed comprehensive training programs that covered various aspects of the business.

These training programs included:

- Product Knowledge: Consultants were trained extensively on the features, benefits, and usage of Mary Kay products. This knowledge empowered them to confidently recommend products and provide valuable beauty advice to customers.

- Sales Techniques: Training sessions focused on effective sales techniques, including how to approach potential customers, conduct product demonstrations, and close sales. Role-playing exercises and practical scenarios helped consultants develop their skills.

- Customer Service: Consultants were taught the principles of exceptional customer service, including how to listen to customer needs, provide personalized recommendations, and handle complaints professionally.

- Business Management: Training also included guidance on managing their independent businesses, such as setting goals, managing finances, and organizing inventory.

3. Ongoing Education and Development

Mary Kay Ash believed in the importance of continuous learning and development. To ensure that consultants remained motivated and updated on the latest trends, the company provided ongoing education opportunities.

Regular workshops, seminars, and conferences were organized to introduce new products, share best practices, and offer advanced training on various topics. These events also served as platforms for networking and building camaraderie among consultants.

4. Mentorship Programs

Mentorship was a key component of Mary Kay's training strategy. Experienced consultants and leaders were encouraged to mentor new recruits, providing guidance, support, and encouragement. This mentorship helped new consultants navigate the challenges of the business and accelerate their growth.

Mentorship programs fostered a sense of community and belonging, creating a supportive environment where consultants could learn from each other's experiences and successes.

Motivational Techniques

Mary Kay Ash was a master of motivation, using various techniques to inspire her salesforce and keep them engaged and committed to their goals. Her motivational strategies were designed to foster a sense of achievement, recognition, and personal growth.

1. Recognition and Rewards

Recognition and rewards were integral to Mary Kay's motivational strategy. Mary Kay Ash believed that acknowledging and celebrating achievements motivated individuals and fostered a sense of pride and loyalty. The company implemented various recognition programs to celebrate the accomplishments of its beauty consultants.

Awards and Ceremonies: Consultants who reached sales milestones, recruited new team members, or demonstrated exceptional leadership were honored and celebrated at company events and ceremonies. These events provided public recognition and reinforced the company's values.

Incentives and Prizes: Mary Kay Cosmetics offered a range of incentives and prizes, including luxury items, travel opportunities, and the iconic pink Cadillac. These rewards were visible symbols of success and inspired many consultants to strive for excellence.

2. Goal Setting and Achievement

Mary Kay Ash emphasized the importance of setting and achieving goals. Consultants were encouraged to set specific, measurable, achievable, relevant, and time-bound (SMART) goals for their businesses. This practice helped consultants stay focused and motivated.

Regular goal-setting workshops and coaching sessions were organized to assist consultants in defining their goals and developing action plans. Celebrating the achievement of these goals provided a sense of accomplishment and motivation to aim higher.

3. Personal Growth and Development

Mary Kay Ash believed that personal growth and development were essential for long-term success. The company provided opportunities for consultants to develop their skills, build confidence, and enhance their self-esteem.

Personal development programs included leadership training, public speaking workshops, and self-improvement seminars. These programs empowered consultants to take on new challenges and grow both personally and professionally.

4. Positive Reinforcement

Mary Kay Ash's leadership style was characterized by positive reinforcement. She focused on recognizing strengths and providing constructive feedback. This approach created a positive and supportive environment where consultants felt valued and encouraged.

Positive reinforcement was reinforced through regular communication, such as personalized notes, phone calls, and public acknowledgments. This consistent encouragement helped consultants stay motivated and committed to their goals.

5. Building a Sense of Community

Mary Kay Ash fostered a strong sense of community within the company. Regular events, conferences, and meetings provided opportunities for consultants to connect, share experiences, and celebrate achievements together. This sense of community created a supportive network that motivated consultants to stay engaged and committed.

Customer Service Excellence

Exceptional customer service was a hallmark of Mary Kay Cosmetics. Mary Kay Ash believed that providing outstanding service was essential for building customer loyalty and ensuring long-term success. Her strategies for achieving customer service excellence included personalized attention, high-quality products, and a commitment to customer satisfaction.

1. Personalized Attention

Mary Kay Ash understood the importance of personalized attention in building strong customer relationships. Beauty consultants were trained to provide one-on-one consultations, tailored product recommendations, and personalized beauty advice. This personalized service created a more meaningful and memorable experience for customers.

Consultants were encouraged to listen to their customers, understand their needs, and provide solutions that genuinely addressed their concerns. This empathetic approach helped build trust and rapport with customers.

2. High-Quality Products

Mary Kay Ash was committed to offering high-quality products that delivered real benefits to customers. The company invested in research and development to create innovative and effective beauty products. Consultants were trained extensively on the features, benefits, and usage of these products, empowering them to confidently recommend products to their customers.

The quality of Mary Kay products was a key factor in building customer loyalty and satisfaction. Customers who experienced positive results with Mary Kay products were more likely to return and make repeat purchases.

3. Commitment to Customer Satisfaction

Customer satisfaction was a top priority for Mary Kay Cosmetics. The company implemented policies and practices to ensure that customers were satisfied with their purchases and experiences.

Satisfaction Guarantee: Mary Kay Cosmetics offered a satisfaction guarantee on all products, allowing customers to return or exchange products if they were not satisfied. This policy provided customers with peace of mind and reinforced the company's commitment to quality.

Responsive Customer Support: Consultants were trained to handle customer inquiries, complaints, and feedback professionally and promptly. Providing responsive and helpful customer support was essential for maintaining customer satisfaction and loyalty.

4. Creating Positive Experiences

Mary Kay Ash believed in creating positive and memorable experiences for customers. Consultants were encouraged to organize events, workshops, and parties where customers could gather, learn about beauty tips, and try new products. These events fostered a sense of community and connection, enhancing the overall customer experience.

Creating positive experiences extended beyond product interactions. Consultants were trained to show appreciation to customers through thank-you notes, small gifts, and special offers. These gestures of appreciation made customers feel valued and strengthened their loyalty to the brand.

5. Building Long-Term Relationships

Building long-term relationships with customers was a priority for Mary Kay consultants. Instead of focusing solely on short-term sales, consultants aimed to develop lasting connections with their customers. This long-term approach fostered trust, loyalty, and mutual respect.

Consultants regularly followed up with their customers, providing updates on new products, promotions, and beauty tips. This ongoing communication kept customers engaged and informed, reinforcing their connection to the brand.

Legacy and Lasting Impact on Direct Sales Marketing

Mary Kay Ash's innovative strategies and commitment to empowering women through direct sales have left an enduring legacy in the business world. Her influence extends beyond Mary Kay Cosmetics, shaping the practices of other businesses and continuing to inspire entrepreneurs and leaders. This section explores her innovations in direct sales, her influence on other businesses, and the ongoing mission of Mary Kay Cosmetics.

Innovations in Direct Sales

Mary Kay Ash introduced several groundbreaking innovations that revolutionized the direct sales industry. Her approach to direct sales was characterized by empowerment, recognition, and personalized service, setting new standards for the industry.

1. The Beauty Consultant Model

One of Mary Kay Ash's most significant innovations was the creation of the beauty consultant model. Instead of relying on traditional retail channels, Mary Kay Cosmetics empowered women to become independent beauty consultants who sold products directly to customers. This model provided women with flexible work opportunities and the potential for financial independence.

The beauty consultant model emphasized personalized service, allowing consultants to build strong relationships with their customers. This approach not only enhanced customer satisfaction but also created a loyal customer base that trusted and valued the personalized attention they received.

2. Recognition and Rewards Programs

Mary Kay Ash's innovative recognition and rewards programs became a hallmark of the company's culture. By publicly acknowledging and celebrating achievements, she motivated consultants to strive for excellence. The iconic pink Cadillac, awarded to top-performing consultants, became a symbol of success and aspiration within the company.

These recognition programs created a positive and motivating environment where consultants felt valued and appreciated. The emphasis on recognition and rewards inspired other direct sales companies to implement similar programs to motivate and retain their salesforces.

3. Empowerment and Personal Development

Mary Kay Ash's focus on empowerment and personal development set her company apart from others in the industry. She believed in providing opportunities for women to grow both personally and professionally. The comprehensive training programs, mentorship opportunities, and personal development initiatives she implemented helped consultants build confidence and develop valuable skills.

This emphasis on empowerment and personal development has influenced other direct sales companies to prioritize training and support for their salesforces, recognizing that investing in their people leads to long-term success.

4. Customer-Centric Approach

Mary Kay Ash's commitment to customer service excellence and personalized attention was a key innovation in the direct sales industry. By focusing on understanding and meeting customer needs, Mary Kay Cosmetics built strong and lasting relationships with its customers.

This customer-centric approach has become a standard practice in the direct sales industry, with companies recognizing the importance of providing exceptional service and personalized experiences to build customer loyalty and drive business growth.

Influence on Other Businesses

Mary Kay Ash's success and innovative strategies have had a lasting impact on other businesses, both within and outside the direct sales industry. Her principles and practices have been adopted by various companies seeking to empower their workforces, build strong customer relationships, and create positive and motivating cultures.

1. Empowerment and Flexible Work Opportunities

Mary Kay Ash's philosophy of empowering women and providing flexible work opportunities has inspired other businesses to adopt similar approaches. Companies in various industries have recognized the benefits of offering flexible work arrangements, allowing employees to balance their careers with personal responsibilities.

The focus on empowerment and personal development has also influenced businesses to invest in training and support programs that help employees grow and succeed. By creating environments where individuals feel valued and supported, companies can enhance employee satisfaction and retention.

2. Recognition and Rewards Programs

The success of Mary Kay's recognition and rewards programs has demonstrated the power of acknowledging and celebrating achievements. Many companies have implemented similar programs to motivate and engage their employees. By providing meaningful recognition and rewards, businesses can foster a positive and motivating culture that drives performance and loyalty.

3. Customer-Centric Strategies

Mary Kay Ash's customer-centric approach has influenced businesses across industries to prioritize customer satisfaction and personalized service. Companies have recognized that understanding and meeting customer needs is essential for building loyalty and driving business growth.

The emphasis on creating positive and memorable experiences for customers has become a standard practice, with businesses seeking to differentiate themselves through exceptional service and personalized interactions.

4. Direct Sales and Entrepreneurial Opportunities

Mary Kay Ash's innovative beauty consultant model has inspired other direct sales companies to adopt similar approaches. By offering entrepreneurial opportunities and flexible work arrangements, direct sales companies can attract and retain motivated individuals who are passionate about building their businesses.

The success of Mary Kay Cosmetics has demonstrated the potential of the direct sales model to create financial independence and personal growth opportunities for individuals. This has encouraged the growth of the direct sales industry and the adoption of similar models by other companies.

Continuing the Mission

The mission of Mary Kay Ash and the principles she established continue to guide Mary Kay Cosmetics and inspire its consultants and leaders. The company's commitment to empowering women, providing exceptional service, and fostering a positive and supportive culture remains central to its success.

1. Empowering Women Worldwide

Mary Kay Cosmetics continues to empower women worldwide by providing entrepreneurial opportunities and support. The company operates in more than 40 countries, offering women the chance to build their businesses, achieve financial independence, and develop valuable skills.

The company's commitment to empowerment is reflected in its training programs, mentorship opportunities, and recognition initiatives. By continuing to invest in the development and success of its beauty consultants, Mary Kay Cosmetics upholds Mary Kay Ash's legacy of empowerment and personal growth.

2. Commitment to Customer Service Excellence

Mary Kay Cosmetics remains dedicated to providing exceptional customer service and personalized attention. The company's customer-centric approach ensures that customers receive high-quality products, personalized recommendations, and outstanding service.

The satisfaction guarantee, responsive customer support, and ongoing communication with customers reflect the company's commitment to maintaining strong and lasting relationships. By prioritizing customer satisfaction, Mary Kay Cosmetics continues to build loyalty and trust.

3. Innovation and Adaptation

Mary Kay Cosmetics continues to innovate and adapt to changing market trends and customer preferences. The company invests in research and development to create innovative and effective beauty products that meet the evolving needs of its customers.

In addition to product innovation, Mary Kay Cosmetics embraces digital tools and platforms to enhance the consultant and customer experience. The company's e-commerce platform, social media presence, and digital marketing strategies reflect its commitment to staying current and relevant in the digital age.

4. Philanthropy and Social Responsibility

Mary Kay Ash's commitment to giving back to the community lives on through the Mary Kay Ash Charitable Foundation. The foundation supports causes related to cancer research and domestic violence prevention, reflecting the company's dedication to making a positive difference in the lives of women and their families.

Mary Kay Cosmetics also engages in various philanthropic and social responsibility initiatives, including environmental sustainability efforts and community outreach programs. These initiatives demonstrate the company's commitment to creating a better world and continuing Mary Kay Ash's legacy of compassion and generosity.

Mary Kay Ash's strategies for building a loyal salesforce and customer base, her innovative contributions to direct sales, and her lasting impact on the business world have left an indelible mark on the industry. Her commitment to empowering women, recognizing and celebrating achievements, and providing exceptional customer service set new standards for success.

The principles and practices established by Mary Kay Ash continue to guide Mary Kay Cosmetics and inspire other businesses. Her legacy of empowerment, innovation, and customer-centricity serves as a beacon for entrepreneurs and leaders seeking to create positive and impactful businesses.

Mary Kay Ash's life and work are a testament to the transformative power of vision, determination, and a commitment to helping others succeed. Her enduring influence reminds us that by empowering individuals, fostering a supportive culture, and prioritizing customer satisfaction, we can achieve greatness and make a meaningful difference in the world.

Chapter 5:

Seth Godin
The Modern Marketing Guru

Seth Godin is widely recognized as one of the most influential figures in modern marketing. His innovative ideas, thought-provoking publications, and extensive contributions to the field have reshaped how businesses and marketers approach their work. This section delves into Godin's career overview and achievements, his major publications and ideas, and his profound influence on the marketing industry.

Early Life and Education

Seth Godin was born on July 10, 1960, in Mount Vernon, New York. He attended Tufts University, where he earned a degree in computer science and philosophy. This unique combination of technical and philosophical training would later inform his approach to marketing, blending analytical rigor with deep insights into human behavior.

After graduating from Tufts, Godin went on to earn his MBA from the Stanford Graduate School of Business. His time at Stanford exposed him to the cutting-edge thinking and entrepreneurial spirit that would shape his career.

Early Career and Entrepreneurship

Godin's professional journey began at Spinnaker Software, where he worked as a brand manager. However, his entrepreneurial spirit soon led him to strike out on his own. In 1986, he founded Seth Godin Productions, a book packaging business. While the company achieved moderate success, Godin's real breakthrough came with his next venture.

In 1995, Godin founded Yoyodyne, a pioneering interactive direct marketing company. Yoyodyne used innovative techniques to engage consumers, such as online contests and games, to build email lists and drive marketing campaigns. This early foray into digital marketing showcased Godin's ability to leverage emerging technologies to create new marketing paradigms.

Yoyodyne's success caught the attention of Yahoo!, which acquired the company in 1998 for approximately $30 million. Following the acquisition, Godin joined Yahoo! as Vice President of Direct Marketing, where he continued to innovate and push the boundaries of digital marketing.

Author and Thought Leader

After leaving Yahoo!, Godin focused on writing and sharing his ideas on marketing and business. His work has since become a cornerstone of modern marketing thought, influencing countless professionals and organizations worldwide.

Major Publications and Ideas

Seth Godin has authored numerous best-selling books and publications that have introduced groundbreaking concepts and ideas to the marketing world. His work emphasizes the importance of permission marketing, the power of remarkable products, and the need for authenticity and trust in marketing.

1. Permission Marketing

One of Godin's most influential ideas is "permission marketing," a concept he introduced in his 1999 book, "Permission Marketing: Turning Strangers into Friends and Friends into Customers." In contrast to traditional "interruption marketing," where advertisers push their messages to a broad audience, permission marketing focuses on obtaining consent from consumers before delivering marketing messages.

Godin argued that by respecting consumers' attention and building relationships based on trust and mutual interest, marketers could achieve higher engagement and loyalty. Permission marketing involves offering something valuable to consumers, such as information or entertainment, in exchange for their permission to receive further communications.

This concept has become a foundational principle in digital marketing, underpinning strategies such as email marketing, content marketing, and social media engagement. By prioritizing consent and relevance, businesses can create more meaningful and effective marketing campaigns.

2. Purple Cow

In his 2003 book, "Purple Cow: Transform Your Business by Being Remarkable," Godin introduced the idea that businesses need to create products and services that are truly remarkable to stand out in a crowded marketplace. He used the metaphor of a "purple cow" to illustrate that ordinary products blend into the background, while remarkable ones capture attention and drive word-of-mouth.

Godin argued that traditional marketing strategies were no longer sufficient in an age of information overload. Instead, businesses needed to innovate and create products that were worth talking about. This concept of "remarkability" has inspired countless businesses to rethink their offerings and strive for excellence and uniqueness.

3. Tribes

In "Tribes: We Need You to Lead Us" (2008), Godin explored the power of leadership and community in the modern world. He argued that people are naturally drawn to tribes—groups of individuals with shared interests and values. Marketers and business leaders can harness this tribal instinct by creating communities around their brands and leading these groups with authenticity and passion.

Godin emphasized that leadership is not about authority but about the ability to connect and inspire. By building and nurturing tribes, businesses can foster loyalty, engagement, and advocacy. This idea has had a profound impact on social media marketing and community-building strategies.

4. Linchpin

In "Linchpin: Are You Indispensable?" (2010), Godin encouraged individuals to become indispensable in their organizations by embracing creativity, innovation, and personal responsibility. He argued that in the modern economy, success depends on being a "linchpin"—someone who makes a significant impact and contributes uniquely to their work.

Godin's message resonated with professionals seeking to differentiate themselves in a competitive job market. By cultivating their unique talents and taking initiative, individuals can achieve greater fulfillment and success in their careers.

5. The Icarus Deception

In "The Icarus Deception: How High Will You Fly?" (2012), Godin challenged the conventional wisdom that playing it safe is the path to success. He drew on the Greek myth of Icarus, who was warned not to fly too high or too low, to illustrate that in today's world, the real risk lies in not taking risks.

Godin argued that the industrial age mindset of conformity and compliance no longer applies in the modern economy. Instead, success comes from embracing creativity, taking bold risks, and pursuing meaningful work. This message has inspired many to break free from traditional constraints and pursue their passions.

Influence on the Marketing Industry

Seth Godin's contributions have had a profound and lasting impact on the marketing industry. His ideas have reshaped how businesses approach marketing, emphasizing authenticity, engagement, and the creation of value. Several key aspects of his influence include:

1. Shift to Permission Marketing

Godin's concept of permission marketing has fundamentally changed how marketers think about consumer engagement. By prioritizing consent and relevance, businesses have moved away from intrusive advertising methods and embraced strategies that build trust and relationships.

Email marketing, content marketing, and social media engagement are all grounded in the principles of permission marketing. Marketers now focus on delivering valuable content that attracts and retains an audience, leading to higher engagement and loyalty.

2. Emphasis on Remarkability

The idea of creating remarkable products and services has driven businesses to innovate and differentiate themselves in the marketplace. Godin's "Purple Cow" concept has inspired countless companies to rethink their offerings and strive for excellence and uniqueness.

This emphasis on remarkability has led to the development of iconic products and brands that stand out and capture consumer attention. Businesses now recognize that in a crowded market, being ordinary is not an option; they must strive to be extraordinary.

3. Community and Tribe Building

Godin's insights into the power of tribes and community have influenced how businesses approach brand building and customer engagement. By fostering communities around their brands, businesses can create loyal and passionate advocates who drive word-of-mouth and organic growth.

Social media platforms have become key tools for tribe building, allowing brands to connect with their audiences and create meaningful interactions. This approach has shifted the focus from transactional marketing to relationship marketing, where the emphasis is on building long-term connections.

4. Encouragement of Creativity and Innovation

Godin's work has consistently championed the importance of creativity, innovation, and taking risks. His messages in "Linchpin" and "The Icarus Deception" have inspired professionals and entrepreneurs to embrace their unique talents and pursue their passions.

This encouragement of creativity and innovation has led to a more dynamic and entrepreneurial business environment. Individuals and organizations are more willing to experiment, take risks, and push the boundaries of what is possible.

5. Thought Leadership and Education

Seth Godin's extensive body of work, including his books, blog, and public speaking, has positioned him as a leading thought leader in the marketing industry. His insights and ideas continue to shape the discourse around marketing, business, and leadership.

Godin's commitment to education is evident in his creation of the altMBA, an intensive online workshop designed to help professionals develop their leadership and problem-solving skills. This program reflects his belief in the power of education to drive personal and professional growth.

6. Influence on Digital Marketing Practices

Godin's early adoption of digital marketing and his understanding of its potential have influenced the evolution of digital marketing practices. His work at Yoyodyne and Yahoo! demonstrated the power of digital tools to engage consumers and drive marketing success.

Today, digital marketing strategies such as email marketing, content marketing, and social media marketing all draw on principles that Godin championed. His focus on building relationships, delivering value, and respecting consumer attention remains central to effective digital marketing.

Seth Godin's career and contributions to marketing

have left an indelible mark on the industry. His innovative ideas, major publications, and influence on marketing practices have reshaped how businesses engage with consumers and approach their work. Godin's emphasis on permission marketing, remarkability, community building, and creativity has inspired countless professionals and organizations to rethink their strategies and strive for excellence.

Godin's legacy as a modern marketing guru is evident in the widespread adoption of his principles and the enduring relevance of his ideas. As the marketing landscape continues to evolve, his insights will remain a guiding light for those seeking to create meaningful connections, deliver value, and make a lasting impact. Seth Godin's work reminds us that marketing is not just about selling products; it is about building relationships, inspiring change, and making a difference in the world.

Understanding Permission Marketing

Seth Godin's concept of permission marketing has been a transformative idea in the world of marketing. By shifting the focus from traditional interruption-based advertising to building relationships based on trust and consent, Godin has provided a framework that aligns more closely with the preferences and behaviors of modern consumers. This section explores the concept of permission marketing, the shift from interruption to engagement, and the importance of building trust and consent.

The Concept of Permission Marketing

Permission marketing is a marketing approach that seeks to obtain the consumer's consent before delivering marketing messages. Instead of bombarding consumers with unsolicited advertisements, permission marketing involves creating a value exchange where consumers willingly opt-in to receive communications.

Key Principles of Permission Marketing:

- Respect for Consumer Attention: Permission marketing acknowledges that consumer attention is a valuable and limited resource. By seeking permission, marketers show respect for the consumer's time and attention.

- Value Exchange: To obtain permission, marketers must offer something of value in return. This could be useful information, entertainment, discounts, or other incentives that make the consumer willing to engage.

- Relevance and Personalization: Permission marketing relies on delivering relevant and personalized content that meets the consumer's interests and needs. This relevance enhances the likelihood of engagement and builds a stronger relationship.

- Ongoing Relationship: Permission marketing is not a one-time interaction but an ongoing relationship. Marketers must continually provide value to maintain the consumer's interest and trust.

Benefits of Permission Marketing:

- Higher Engagement Rates: Since consumers have willingly opted-in, they are more likely to engage with the marketing messages they receive.

- Improved Customer Relationships: By focusing on consent and value, permission marketing helps build stronger, more trust-based relationships with customers.

- Better Targeting: Permission marketing allows for more precise targeting, as marketers can segment their audience based on the information provided during the opt-in process.

- Reduced Costs: Because permission marketing is more targeted, it can be more cost-effective than broad, interruption-based advertising campaigns.

Shifting from Interruption to Engagement

Traditional advertising methods, such as television commercials, radio ads, and pop-up banners, are often referred to as interruption marketing. These methods interrupt the consumer's activities to deliver a message, often leading to annoyance and ad fatigue. Permission marketing, on the other hand, focuses on engagement rather than interruption.

Challenges of Interruption Marketing:

- Ad Blindness: Consumers have become adept at ignoring ads, leading to reduced effectiveness of interruption-based marketing.

- Negative Perception: Unsolicited ads can create a negative perception of the brand, as they are often seen as intrusive and annoying.

- Inefficiency: Interruption marketing casts a wide net, reaching many uninterested consumers and resulting in low conversion rates.

Strategies for Engagement:

- Content Marketing: Creating valuable and relevant content that attracts and engages the target audience. This can include blog posts, videos, infographics, and social media content.

- Email Marketing: Building an email list through opt-ins and sending personalized, relevant emails to subscribers. This keeps the audience engaged and informed about new products, offers, and updates.

- Social Media Engagement: Using social media platforms to interact with the audience, respond to comments, and share engaging content. Social media allows for two-way communication, fostering a sense of community.

- Interactive Campaigns: Developing campaigns that encourage participation, such as quizzes, contests, and user-generated content. Interactive elements increase engagement and make the experience more memorable.

Case Study:

A notable example of shifting from interruption to engagement is HubSpot. The company uses content marketing to attract and engage its audience. By providing valuable resources such as eBooks, webinars, and blog posts, HubSpot builds trust and establishes itself as an authority in the marketing and sales space. This approach has helped HubSpot grow its customer base and maintain high levels of engagement.

Building Trust and Consent

Trust and consent are foundational to permission marketing. Without them, the relationship between the brand and the consumer is likely to be weak and short-lived. Building trust and obtaining consent require a strategic approach that prioritizes transparency, honesty, and value.

Strategies for Building Trust:

- Transparency: Being open and honest about how consumer data will be used and ensuring that privacy policies are clear and accessible. Transparency helps build confidence in the brand.

- Consistent Value: Continuously providing valuable content and offers that meet the consumer's needs and expectations. Consistency reinforces trust and keeps the audience engaged.

- Authenticity: Communicating in an authentic and genuine manner. Brands that are perceived as authentic are more likely to build strong relationships with their audience.

- Responsiveness: Being responsive to customer inquiries, feedback, and concerns. Prompt and helpful responses demonstrate that the brand values its customers and is committed to their satisfaction.

Obtaining Consent:

- Clear Opt-In Processes: Implementing clear and straightforward opt-in processes where consumers explicitly agree to receive communications. This can include email sign-ups, subscription forms, and social media follows.

- Double Opt-In: Using a double opt-in process where consumers confirm their subscription through a follow-up email. This ensures that only genuinely interested individuals are added to the mailing list.

- Opt-Out Options: Providing easy and accessible opt-out options for consumers who no longer wish to receive communications.

Respecting the consumer's choice to opt-out is crucial for maintaining trust.

- Incentives for Opt-In: Offering incentives such as discounts, free trials, or exclusive content to encourage consumers to opt-in. Incentives can make the value exchange clear and compelling.

Case Study:

A successful example of building trust and consent is Apple. The company prioritizes user privacy and data security, making it a central part of its value proposition. Apple's transparent privacy policies, secure data handling practices, and consistent delivery of high-quality products and services have earned it a high level of trust among consumers.

The Concept of Tribes and Community Building

Seth Godin's concept of tribes and community building has had a profound impact on modern marketing. By focusing on the power of small, connected groups and the importance of leadership, Godin has provided a framework for creating loyal and engaged communities around brands. This section explores the definition and leadership of tribes, the importance of community, and case studies of successful tribe-building.

Defining and Leading Tribes

A tribe, as defined by Seth Godin, is a group of people connected to one another, a leader, and an idea.

Tribes are driven by shared interests, values, and goals, and they thrive on the connections between members. Leading a tribe involves inspiring and guiding the group, fostering a sense of belonging and purpose.

Key Elements of Tribes:

- Connection: Members of a tribe are connected to one another through shared interests and values. These connections create a sense of community and belonging.

- Leadership: Effective tribes have a leader who inspires, guides, and motivates the members. Leadership is about facilitating connections and driving the tribe towards a common goal.

- Shared Idea: Tribes are united by a shared idea or purpose. This idea provides a sense of direction and meaning for the group.

Leadership Strategies:

- Inspiration: Leaders must inspire their tribes by communicating a compelling vision and demonstrating passion and commitment.

  - Inspirational leaders motivate members to take action and contribute to the tribe's goals.

- Facilitation: Leaders facilitate connections within the tribe by creating opportunities for interaction and collaboration. This can include organizing events, creating online forums, and encouraging member contributions.

- Empowerment: Effective leaders empower tribe members by giving them a voice and encouraging their participation. Empowered members are more likely to be engaged and committed to the tribe.

- Authenticity: Authentic leadership builds trust and credibility. Leaders must be genuine, transparent, and consistent in their actions and communications.

Case Study:

A prominent example of successful tribe leadership is Elon Musk and the community he has built around Tesla. Musk's vision for sustainable energy and electric vehicles has inspired a passionate and loyal following. Through his leadership, Musk has fostered a strong sense of community among Tesla owners and enthusiasts, who share a commitment to innovation and sustainability.

The Importance of Community

Community is a powerful force in marketing. It creates a sense of belonging, fosters loyalty, and drives engagement. Building and nurturing a community around a brand can lead to long-term success and a competitive advantage.

Benefits of Community Building:

- Loyalty and Advocacy: Members of a community are more likely to be loyal to the brand and advocate for it within their networks. This can lead to increased word-of-mouth marketing and organic growth.

- Engagement: Communities provide a platform for ongoing engagement with the brand. Members are more likely to participate in discussions, provide feedback, and contribute content.

- Support and Collaboration: Communities offer support and collaboration opportunities for members. They can share experiences, solve problems, and provide recommendations, enhancing the overall brand experience.

- Customer Insights: Building a community allows brands to gain valuable insights into customer preferences, behaviors, and needs. This information can inform product development, marketing strategies, and customer service improvements.

Strategies for Building a Community:

- Creating a Shared Space: Establishing a shared space where community members can interact is essential. This can be an online forum, a social media group, or a dedicated website. The space should be user-friendly and facilitate meaningful interactions.

- Encouraging Participation: Actively encouraging participation helps build a vibrant and engaged community. Brands can prompt discussions, ask questions, and create opportunities for members to share their experiences and insights.

- Providing Value: Consistently providing value to the community is crucial. This can include exclusive content, special offers, and access to events. By delivering value, brands reinforce the benefits of being part of the community.

- Fostering Connections: Facilitating connections between community members enhances the sense of belonging. Brands can organize meetups, virtual events, and collaborative projects to bring members together.

- Recognizing Contributions: Recognizing and celebrating member contributions builds a positive and supportive community culture. Brands can highlight member achievements, feature user-generated content, and offer rewards for active participation.

Case Study:

LEGO is a prime example of successful community building. The LEGO Ideas platform allows fans to submit their own designs for potential LEGO sets. The community votes on submissions, and winning designs are produced as official LEGO sets. This approach not only fosters creativity and engagement but also strengthens the bond between LEGO and its fans.

Case Studies of Successful Tribe-Building

Several brands have successfully built tribes and communities, leveraging the power of connection and shared purpose to drive their success. These case studies illustrate different approaches to tribe-building and highlight the benefits of fostering a loyal and engaged community.

1. Harley-Davidson: The Harley Owners Group (HOG)

Harley-Davidson has built a strong tribe around its brand through the Harley Owners Group (HOG). HOG is an exclusive community for Harley-Davidson motorcycle owners, offering a range of benefits, including events, rides, and merchandise.

Key Strategies:

- Exclusive Membership: Membership in HOG is exclusive to Harley-Davidson owners, creating a sense of belonging and pride.

- Events and Rides: HOG organizes events and rides that bring members together, fostering camaraderie and shared experiences.

- Brand Advocacy: HOG members are passionate advocates for the brand, promoting Harley-Davidson within their networks and participating in brand-related activities.

Benefits:

- Loyalty and Advocacy: HOG members are highly loyal to Harley-Davidson and actively advocate for the brand.

- Engagement: The community provides ongoing engagement opportunities, enhancing the overall brand experience.

- Customer Insights: Harley-Davidson gains valuable insights into customer preferences and behaviors through its interactions with HOG members.

2. CrossFit: The CrossFit Community

CrossFit has built a global community of fitness enthusiasts who share a commitment to the CrossFit methodology and lifestyle. The community is characterized by strong connections, mutual support, and a shared sense of purpose.

Key Strategies:

- Local Affiliates: CrossFit gyms (affiliates) serve as local hubs for the community, offering a space for members to train, connect, and support each other.

- Events and Competitions: CrossFit organizes events and competitions, such as the CrossFit Games, that bring the community together and celebrate achievements.

- Content and Resources: CrossFit provides a

wealth of content and resources, including workout plans, nutritional advice, and educational materials, to support members in their fitness journeys.

Benefits:

- Loyalty and Advocacy: CrossFit members are highly dedicated to the brand and advocate for it within their networks.

- Engagement: The community offers ongoing engagement opportunities, enhancing the overall brand experience.

- Customer Insights: CrossFit gains valuable insights into member preferences and behaviors through its interactions with the community.

3. Nike: The Nike+ Community

Nike has successfully built a tribe around its Nike+ platform, which connects runners and athletes through technology and shared experiences. The community is characterized by strong connections, mutual support, and a shared commitment to fitness and performance.

Key Strategies:

- Technology Integration: The Nike+ platform integrates with wearable devices and apps, allowing members to track their progress and connect with others.

- Challenges and Events: Nike+ organizes challenges and events that encourage members to set goals, compete, and celebrate achievements.

- Content and Resources: Nike+ provides a wealth of content and resources, including training plans, motivational content, and expert advice, to support members in their fitness journeys.

Benefits:

- Loyalty and Advocacy: Nike+ members are highly dedicated to the brand and advocate for it within their networks.

- Engagement: The community offers ongoing engagement opportunities, enhancing the overall brand experience.

- Customer Insights: Nike gains valuable insights into member preferences and behaviors through its interactions with the Nike+ community.

Seth Godin's concepts of permission marketing and tribe-building have had a profound impact on the marketing industry. By focusing on obtaining consent, building trust, and creating value, permission marketing offers a more effective and respectful approach to engaging with consumers. The shift from interruption to engagement has led to higher engagement rates, improved customer relationships, and better-targeted marketing efforts.

The concept of tribes and community building emphasizes the power of connection, leadership, and shared purpose. Successful tribe-building strategies foster loyalty, engagement, and advocacy, driving long-term success for brands. By creating and nurturing communities, businesses can gain valuable insights, support customer needs, and build strong, lasting relationships.

Seth Godin's ideas continue to inspire and guide marketers, emphasizing the importance of authenticity, trust, and meaningful connections in achieving marketing excellence. As the marketing landscape evolves, these principles remain relevant and essential for building successful and impactful brands.

The Importance of Authenticity and Storytelling

In today's marketing landscape, authenticity and storytelling are crucial for building meaningful connections with audiences. Consumers are increasingly seeking brands that resonate with their values and communicate honestly. This section explores the importance of crafting authentic stories, connecting with audiences on a deeper level, and provides examples of effective storytelling.
Crafting Authentic Stories

Authenticity in storytelling is about being genuine, transparent, and true to the brand's values and mission. Authentic stories resonate with audiences because they reflect real experiences, emotions, and beliefs. Here are some strategies for crafting authentic stories:

1. Understand Your Brand's Core Values

Before crafting stories, it's essential to have a deep understanding of your brand's core values and mission. These elements should be at the heart of every story you tell. Authentic storytelling aligns with these values and reinforces the brand's identity.

2. Focus on Real Experiences

Authentic stories often stem from real experiences, whether they are those of the brand's founders, employees, or customers. Sharing genuine experiences creates a sense of relatability and trust. For example, a brand might share the founder's journey and challenges in starting the business, or highlight customer testimonials and success stories.

3. Emphasize Transparency

Transparency is key to authenticity. Being open about the brand's practices, challenges, and journey builds trust with the audience. This includes acknowledging mistakes and showing how the brand has learned and grown from them. Transparency demonstrates that the brand is honest and accountable.

4. Use a Consistent Voice

Consistency in voice and tone across all storytelling efforts ensures that the brand feels cohesive and reliable. Whether the story is shared on social media, in a blog post, or through a video, the brand's voice should remain consistent to reinforce authenticity.

5. Highlight Human Elements

Humanizing the brand by showcasing the people behind it—employees, founders, and customers—adds depth to the stories. Highlighting human elements makes the brand more relatable and personable. This can be achieved through interviews, behind-the-scenes content, and employee spotlights.

6. Engage Emotionally

Authentic stories often evoke emotions. By tapping into universal themes like hope, perseverance, love, and community, brands can create emotional connections with their audience. Emotional engagement helps stories stick and motivates action. Connecting with Audiences on a Deeper Level

Connecting with audiences on a deeper level involves understanding their needs, desires, and values, and crafting stories that resonate with these elements. Here's how brands can achieve this connection:

1. Know Your Audience

Understanding the audience's demographics, psychographics, and behavior is crucial. Conducting research, surveys, and using data analytics can provide insights into what matters to the audience. This knowledge helps tailor stories that align with their interests and values.

2. Address Audience Pain Points

Effective storytelling often addresses the audience's pain points and challenges. By showing how the brand can solve these problems or improve their lives, stories become more relevant and compelling. For example, a healthcare brand might share stories of patients who overcame health challenges with their products or services.

3. Reflect Audience Values

Aligning the brand's stories with the values and beliefs of the audience strengthens the connection. If the audience values sustainability, for example, the brand can share stories about its eco-friendly practices and initiatives. This alignment fosters a sense of shared purpose and loyalty.

4. Foster a Two-Way Conversation

Engaging the audience in a two-way conversation rather than just broadcasting messages creates a deeper connection. Encouraging feedback, comments, and participation in storytelling fosters a sense of community and involvement. Social media platforms are ideal for this interactive engagement.

5. Create a Sense of Belonging

Storytelling that creates a sense of belonging can turn audiences into loyal advocates. By highlighting the community aspect of the brand, such as customer stories and user-generated content, brands can make audiences feel part of something bigger. This sense of belonging fosters loyalty and advocacy.

6. Use Multi-Channel Storytelling

Utilizing multiple channels to tell stories ensures that the message reaches the audience wherever they are. Combining social media, blogs, videos, podcasts, and other platforms allows for a richer and more engaging storytelling experience. Each channel can offer a unique angle or format to the story.

Examples of Effective Storytelling

1. Dove - Real Beauty Campaign

Dove's Real Beauty campaign is a powerful example of authentic storytelling. Launched in 2004, the campaign aimed to challenge traditional beauty standards and promote body positivity. Dove used real women of diverse shapes, sizes, and ethnicities in its advertisements, rather than professional models.

The campaign's storytelling was rooted in real experiences and emotions. Dove shared stories of women who had been affected by unrealistic beauty standards and showcased their journey towards self-acceptance. This authenticity resonated deeply with audiences and helped build a strong emotional connection with the brand.

2. Nike - Dream Crazy Campaign

Nike's Dream Crazy campaign, featuring former NFL player Colin Kaepernick, is another example of effective storytelling. The campaign focused on the theme of dreaming big and overcoming obstacles, aligning with Nike's core values of inspiration and determination.

By supporting Kaepernick, who had become a polarizing figure for his activism, Nike took a bold stand on social issues. The storytelling was authentic and reflected Nike's commitment to social justice and equality. This resonated with many consumers who shared these values, strengthening their connection to the brand.

3. Airbnb - Belong Anywhere Campaign

Airbnb's Belong Anywhere campaign highlights the importance of community and belonging. The campaign focuses on the experiences of hosts and guests, sharing their stories of connection, cultural exchange, and hospitality.

Airbnb's storytelling emphasizes the human element, showcasing real people and their unique experiences. By doing so, the brand creates a sense of trust and authenticity. The campaign's message of belonging and connection resonates with audiences who value travel and cultural exchange.

4. Patagonia - The Footprint Chronicles

Patagonia's The Footprint Chronicles is an example of transparency and authenticity in storytelling. The initiative provides detailed information about the environmental and social impact of Patagonia's products, including the supply chain and manufacturing processes.

By being transparent about the challenges and efforts to reduce its environmental footprint, Patagonia builds trust with its audience. The storytelling aligns with the brand's values of sustainability and responsibility, resonating with consumers who prioritize ethical consumption.

Case Studies of Successful Campaigns Inspired by Godin's Ideas

Seth Godin's innovative ideas on permission marketing, tribes, and community building have inspired numerous successful marketing campaigns. This section examines real-world applications of permission marketing, successful tribe-led initiatives, and lessons learned from campaigns influenced by Godin's concepts.

Real-World Applications of Permission Marketing

1. HubSpot

HubSpot is a pioneer in inbound marketing, a strategy closely aligned with Seth Godin's concept of permission marketing. Instead of interrupting potential customers with unsolicited ads, HubSpot attracts them with valuable content and engages them through permission-based channels.

Strategy:

- Content Creation: HubSpot produces high-quality content, including blog posts, eBooks, webinars, and videos, that addresses the pain points and interests of its target audience.

- Lead Generation: The content is gated, meaning users must provide their contact information to access it. This opt-in approach ensures that HubSpot builds a database of interested and engaged prospects.

- Email Marketing: HubSpot uses email marketing to nurture these leads, providing additional valuable content and personalized offers. This ongoing engagement builds trust and moves prospects through the sales funnel.

Results:

HubSpot's permission marketing strategy has been highly effective in generating leads, building customer relationships, and driving business growth. By providing value and obtaining consent, HubSpot has created a loyal and engaged customer base.

2. Glossier

Glossier, a beauty brand, uses permission marketing to build strong relationships with its customers. The brand focuses on community-driven content and leverages customer feedback to inform its product development and marketing strategies.

Strategy:

- Community Engagement: Glossier actively engages with its community on social media, encouraging user-generated content and feedback. This interaction creates a sense of involvement and ownership among customers.

- Email Newsletters: Glossier's email newsletters are a key component of its permission marketing strategy. Subscribers receive personalized content, early access to new products, and special promotions.

- Product Development: Glossier involves its community in the product development process, using feedback and suggestions to create products that meet their needs and preferences.

Results:

Glossier's permission marketing approach has fostered a highly engaged and loyal community. By prioritizing customer input and building relationships based on trust and value, Glossier has achieved significant growth and brand loyalty.

Successful Tribe-Led Initiatives

1. Harley-Davidson: The Harley Owners Group (HOG)

Harley-Davidson has successfully built a tribe around its brand through the Harley Owners Group (HOG). This exclusive community for Harley-Davidson owners fosters loyalty and advocacy through shared experiences and a sense of belonging.

Strategy:

- Membership Benefits: HOG members receive exclusive benefits, including access to events, rides, and merchandise. These benefits create a sense of exclusivity and reward loyalty.

- Events and Rides: HOG organizes numerous events and rides, providing opportunities for members to connect and share their passion for Harley-Davidson motorcycles.

- Community Engagement: The community aspect of HOG is emphasized through local chapters and online forums, where members can interact, share experiences, and support each other.

Results:

HOG has created a loyal and passionate tribe that actively promotes the Harley-Davidson brand. The sense of community and belonging fosters strong brand loyalty and advocacy, driving both retention and acquisition.

2. CrossFit: The CrossFit Community

CrossFit has built a global tribe of fitness enthusiasts who share a commitment to the CrossFit methodology and lifestyle. The community is characterized by strong connections, mutual support, and a shared sense of purpose.

Strategy:

- Local Affiliates: CrossFit gyms (affiliates) serve as local hubs for the community, offering a space for members to train, connect, and support each other.

- Events and Competitions: CrossFit organizes events and competitions, such as the CrossFit Games, that bring the community together and celebrate achievements.

- Content and Resources: CrossFit provides a wealth of content and resources, including workout plans, nutritional advice, and educational materials, to support members in their fitness journeys.

Results:

The CrossFit community has created a loyal and dedicated tribe that drives brand advocacy and organic growth. The sense of belonging and shared purpose fosters strong engagement and retention. Lessons Learned from Godin-Inspired Campaigns

1. Prioritize Value and Consent

Permission marketing emphasizes the importance of providing value and obtaining consent. Brands should focus on creating valuable content and experiences that attract and engage their audience. By obtaining consent, brands build trust and create a foundation for long-term relationships.

Example:

HubSpot's inbound marketing strategy prioritizes valuable content and opt-in engagement, leading to high-quality leads and strong customer relationships.

2. Build and Nurture Communities

Building a tribe or community around the brand fosters loyalty, engagement, and advocacy. Brands should focus on creating shared experiences, providing value, and facilitating connections within the community.

Example:

Harley-Davidson's Harley Owners Group (HOG) creates a strong sense of community and belonging, driving loyalty and advocacy.

3. Be Authentic and Transparent

Authenticity and transparency are crucial for building trust and credibility. Brands should be honest about their practices, values, and challenges, and engage with their audience in a genuine manner.

Example:

Patagonia's The Footprint Chronicles demonstrates transparency and authenticity by providing detailed information about the environmental and social impact of its products.

4. Engage Emotionally

Effective storytelling often evokes emotions and connects with the audience on a deeper level. Brands should focus on creating stories that resonate emotionally and reflect the values and experiences of their audience.

Example:

Dove's Real Beauty campaign engages emotionally by challenging traditional beauty standards and promoting body positivity.

5. Foster a Two-Way Conversation

Engaging the audience in a two-way conversation rather than just broadcasting messages creates a deeper connection. Brands should encourage feedback, comments, and participation in storytelling to foster a sense of community and involvement.

Example:

Glossier's community-driven approach encourages user-generated content and feedback, creating a sense of involvement and ownership among customers. Seth Godin's concepts of authenticity, storytelling, permission marketing, and tribe-building have had a profound impact on modern marketing. By focusing on genuine and transparent communication, brands can build meaningful connections with their audiences. Permission marketing emphasizes the importance of consent and value, leading to higher engagement and trust. Building tribes and communities fosters loyalty, advocacy, and long-term success.

Real-world examples and case studies demonstrate the effectiveness of these strategies. Brands like HubSpot, Glossier, Harley-Davidson, and CrossFit have successfully implemented Godin-inspired approaches, creating loyal and engaged customer bases. The lessons learned from these campaigns highlight the importance of prioritizing value, building communities, being authentic, engaging emotionally, and fostering two-way conversations.

As the marketing landscape continues to evolve, Seth Godin's principles provide a timeless framework for creating impactful and sustainable marketing strategies. By embracing authenticity, storytelling, permission marketing, and community building, brands can achieve lasting success and make a meaningful difference in the lives of their customers.

Chapter 6:

Steve Jobs
The Art of Innovation and Branding

Steve Jobs is widely regarded as one of the most influential figures in the technology industry. His visionary approach to innovation and branding not only transformed Apple Inc. into one of the world's most valuable companies but also revolutionized several industries, from personal computing to music and mobile communications. This section explores Jobs' early life and career, the founding of Apple and its key milestones, and his enduring legacy in the tech world.

Early Life

Steve Jobs was born on February 24, 1955, in San Francisco, California, and was adopted by Paul and Clara Jobs. From a young age, Jobs displayed an interest in electronics and gadgets, influenced by his adoptive father, who was a machinist and craftsman. This early exposure to mechanics and craftsmanship would later inform Jobs' meticulous attention to detail and design.

Jobs grew up in the heart of Silicon Valley, which was rapidly becoming the center of the technology universe. He attended Homestead High School in Cupertino, California, where he met Steve Wozniak, a fellow tech enthusiast. Their friendship and shared passion for electronics would eventually lead to the creation of Apple Inc.

Education and Early Career

After high school, Jobs enrolled at Reed College in Portland, Oregon, but dropped out after just one semester. Despite this, he continued to attend classes that interested him, such as calligraphy, which later influenced the typography and design of Apple products.

In 1974, Jobs joined Atari, Inc., as a technician, working alongside Wozniak. During this time, he saved enough money to embark on a spiritual journey to India, where he explored Eastern philosophies and Buddhism. This journey had a profound impact on his perspective and leadership style.

Upon returning to the United States, Jobs and Wozniak began collaborating on a project that would eventually become Apple's first product. They started building and selling "blue boxes," devices that allowed users to make free long-distance phone calls by manipulating telephone signaling. This venture provided them with the initial funds and confidence to pursue larger ambitions.

Founding of Apple and Key Milestones

The Birth of Apple

In 1976, Jobs and Wozniak co-founded Apple Computer, Inc., in the Jobs family garage. Their goal was to make computers more accessible and user-friendly. Their first product, the Apple I, was a single-board computer that lacked a case, keyboard, or monitor. Despite its limitations, the Apple I demonstrated the potential for personal computers and garnered significant interest.

Apple II and Early Success

The release of the Apple II in 1977 marked a significant milestone for the company. Unlike its predecessor, the Apple II was a fully assembled personal computer with a plastic case and a built-in keyboard. It was one of the first computers to feature color graphics and a floppy disk drive. The Apple II's user-friendly design and powerful capabilities made it a commercial success and established Apple as a major player in the emerging personal computer market.

Introduction of the Macintosh

In 1984, Jobs introduced the Macintosh, a groundbreaking computer that featured a graphical user interface (GUI), a mouse, and a sleek design. The Macintosh was a revolutionary product that made computing more intuitive and accessible to a broader audience. The iconic "1984" Super Bowl commercial, directed by Ridley Scott, positioned the Macintosh as a liberating force against the conformity of IBM and the established computer industry.

Despite its innovative design and initial excitement, the Macintosh faced challenges in the market, including high costs and limited software compatibility. These difficulties led to internal conflicts within Apple, and in 1985, Jobs was ousted from the company he co-founded.

NeXT and Pixar

After leaving Apple, Jobs founded NeXT Inc., a company focused on creating high-end workstations for the education and business markets. NeXT's products were known for their advanced technology and elegant design, but they struggled to achieve commercial success. However, the NeXTSTEP operating system would later become the foundation for macOS and iOS.

In 1986, Jobs acquired The Graphics Group, which was later renamed Pixar Animation Studios. Under his leadership, Pixar produced several critically acclaimed and commercially successful animated films, including "Toy Story" (1995), "Finding Nemo" (2003), and "The Incredibles" (2004). Pixar's success established it as a leading animation studio and cemented Jobs' reputation as a visionary leader.

Return to Apple and the Renaissance

In 1996, Apple acquired NeXT, bringing Jobs back to the company as an advisor. By 1997, Jobs had become Apple's interim CEO, and he quickly set about transforming the struggling company. He streamlined Apple's product line, focusing on core products that embodied Apple's design and innovation principles.

iMac and the Revival of Apple

The introduction of the iMac in 1998 marked the beginning of Apple's revival. The iMac featured a distinctive all-in-one design with vibrant colors, making it a standout product in the market. Its simplicity and aesthetic appeal captured consumers' imaginations and significantly boosted Apple's sales.

The Digital Hub Strategy

Jobs envisioned Apple as a "digital hub" for consumers' digital lives, integrating hardware, software, and services. This strategy led to the development of several iconic products and services, including the iPod (2001), iTunes (2001), the iTunes Store (2003), and the iPhone (2007).

iPod and iTunes: Revolutionizing Music

The iPod, a portable digital music player, revolutionized the music industry by making it easy for consumers to carry their entire music libraries with them. The iTunes Store provided a convenient platform for purchasing and downloading music legally. This ecosystem transformed how people consumed music and established Apple as a dominant force in the digital music market.

iPhone: Redefining Mobile Computing

The introduction of the iPhone in 2007 was a watershed moment in the technology industry. The iPhone combined a phone, an iPod, and an internet communicator into a single device with a multi-touch screen interface. It redefined mobile computing and set new standards for smartphones. The iPhone's success propelled Apple to become one of the most valuable companies in the world.

iPad and Beyond

In 2010, Apple introduced the iPad, a tablet computer that further expanded the company's product line and solidified its leadership in consumer electronics. The iPad's intuitive interface and versatile functionality made it a popular choice for both personal and professional use.

Legacy in the Tech World

Design and User Experience

One of Steve Jobs' most enduring legacies is his relentless focus on design and user experience. Jobs believed that technology should be beautiful, intuitive, and accessible. This philosophy drove Apple's product development and resulted in devices that were not only powerful but also a pleasure to use. Apple's emphasis on design has influenced countless other companies and set new standards for the industry.

Integration of Hardware and Software

Jobs championed the integration of hardware and software to create seamless and cohesive user experiences. This approach ensured that Apple's products worked harmoniously, providing users with a consistent and reliable experience. The tight integration of hardware and software became a hallmark of Apple's success and set it apart from competitors.

Branding and Marketing

Steve Jobs was a master of branding and marketing. He understood the importance of creating an emotional connection with consumers and crafting compelling narratives around Apple's products. From iconic advertising campaigns to captivating product launches, Jobs' marketing prowess played a significant role in building Apple's brand and driving its success.

Innovation and Risk-Taking

Jobs' willingness to take risks and pursue bold ideas led to some of the most groundbreaking innovations in the tech industry. He was not afraid to challenge the status quo and push the boundaries of what was possible. This spirit of innovation continues to be a driving force at Apple and has inspired countless entrepreneurs and innovators.

Legacy of Leadership

Steve Jobs' leadership style was characterized by his

vision, passion, and demanding nature. He inspired those around him to strive for excellence and never settle for mediocrity. Jobs' ability to articulate a clear vision and rally his team around it was instrumental in achieving Apple's success.

Enduring Impact

Steve Jobs passed away on October 5, 2011, but his impact on the technology industry continues to be felt. Apple's ongoing success and continued innovation are a testament to his vision and leadership. The products and technologies he helped create have transformed the way we live, work, and communicate.

Cultural Influence

Beyond his contributions to technology, Jobs' influence extends to popular culture. He has been the subject of numerous books, documentaries, and films, and his life and career continue to inspire and fascinate people around the world. Jobs' legacy as a visionary leader and innovator remains a powerful and enduring story.

Philanthropy and Social Impact

While Jobs was known for his business achievements, his impact also extended to philanthropy and social causes. He supported various charitable initiatives and causes, both personally and through Apple. Jobs' commitment to making a positive difference in the world is an important part of his legacy.

Steve Jobs' life and career are a remarkable story of

innovation, resilience, and vision. From his early days building computers in a garage to transforming Apple into a global technology powerhouse, Jobs' impact on the technology industry is unparalleled. His focus on design, user experience, and integration set new standards and inspired countless innovations.

Jobs' ability to create compelling narratives and emotional connections with consumers revolutionized branding and marketing. His willingness to take risks and challenge conventions led to groundbreaking products that have changed the way we live and interact with technology.

Steve Jobs' legacy continues to influence the technology industry and beyond. His vision, leadership, and passion for excellence serve as a guiding light for entrepreneurs and innovators. The products and ideas he brought to life have left an indelible mark on the world, and his story remains an inspiration to all who aspire to make a difference.

Jobs' Approach to Product Design and User Experience

Steve Jobs' approach to product design and user experience was foundational to Apple's success and the profound impact it has had on the technology industry. His relentless focus on simplicity, elegance, and user-centric design set new standards and created some of the most iconic products in history. This section explores Jobs' emphasis on simplicity and elegance, the importance of user experience, and the creation of iconic product designs.
Focus on Simplicity and Elegance

Simplicity as the Ultimate Sophistication

Steve Jobs believed that simplicity was the ultimate sophistication. This philosophy guided every aspect of Apple's product design. Jobs often quoted Leonardo da Vinci, saying, "Simplicity is the ultimate sophistication." This mantra was reflected in Apple's commitment to stripping away unnecessary features and focusing on what truly mattered to users.

Design Principles

Jobs' design principles revolved around clarity, efficiency, and intuitiveness. He pushed his design teams to eliminate clutter and ensure that every element served a clear purpose. This approach resulted in products that were not only visually appealing but also easy to use.

Minimalist Aesthetics

Apple's products are renowned for their minimalist aesthetics. Jobs had a keen eye for design and aesthetics, insisting on clean lines, sleek forms, and the use of high-quality materials. The minimalist design language made Apple's products instantly recognizable and contributed to their premium image.

Attention to Detail

Jobs' meticulous attention to detail was legendary. He was involved in every aspect of product development, from the overall design to the smallest components. This attention to detail ensured that Apple's products were not only functional but also a pleasure to use and behold.

Iterative Design Process

Jobs championed an iterative design process that involved constant refinement and improvement. He believed in prototyping and testing extensively to ensure that the final product was as perfect as possible. This iterative approach allowed Apple to innovate continually and set new benchmarks for quality and performance.

The Importance of User Experience

User-Centric Design

Steve Jobs placed the user at the center of the design process. He believed that technology should serve the user, not the other way around. This user-centric approach was a fundamental shift from the traditional engineering-driven design processes prevalent in the tech industry.

Intuitive Interfaces

One of the hallmarks of Apple's products is their intuitive interfaces. Jobs insisted that products should be easy to use, even for people with no technical background. This focus on intuitiveness led to the development of revolutionary interfaces, such as the graphical user interface (GUI) in the Macintosh and the multi-touch interface in the iPhone.

Seamless Integration
Jobs emphasized the importance of seamless

integration between hardware and software. He believed that by controlling both aspects, Apple could create a cohesive and harmonious user experience. This tight integration ensured that Apple's products worked flawlessly and provided a smooth and consistent experience across different devices.

Accessibility

Accessibility was another key consideration in Jobs' approach to user experience. He believed that technology should be accessible to everyone, regardless of their abilities. Apple invested in developing accessibility features that made their products usable by people with disabilities, further enhancing the user experience.

User Feedback

Jobs valued user feedback and used it to inform product development. Apple actively sought feedback from users through various channels, including surveys, focus groups, and beta testing programs. This feedback loop allowed Apple to understand user needs and preferences better and incorporate them into their products.

Iconic Product Designs

Apple II

The Apple II, introduced in 1977, was one of the first successful personal computers and set the stage for Apple's future innovations. Its user-friendly design, including a built-in keyboard and color graphics, made it accessible to a broader audience. The Apple II's success established Apple as a significant player in the burgeoning personal computer market.

Macintosh

The Macintosh, launched in 1984, was a revolutionary product that introduced the graphical user interface (GUI) to a wider audience. Its iconic design, featuring an all-in-one form factor with a built-in screen, keyboard, and mouse, made it a standout product. The Macintosh's ease of use and innovative interface set new standards for personal computing.

iMac

In 1998, Apple introduced the iMac, a product that played a crucial role in the company's revival. The iMac's distinctive design, with its colorful translucent casing and all-in-one form factor, captured the public's imagination. The iMac was not only a visual departure from traditional computers but also simplified setup and connectivity, enhancing the user experience.

iPod

The iPod, launched in 2001, revolutionized the way people listened to music. Its sleek design, intuitive click wheel interface, and ability to store thousands of songs in a compact device made it a cultural phenomenon. The iPod's success helped reestablish Apple as a leader in consumer electronics and laid the groundwork for future innovations.

iPhone

The iPhone, introduced in 2007, redefined the smartphone industry. Its revolutionary multi-touch interface, elegant design, and seamless integration of phone, iPod, and internet functionalities set a new standard for mobile devices. The iPhone's impact on the tech industry and society as a whole cannot be overstated, as it transformed how people communicate, access information, and interact with technology.

iPad

In 2010, Apple launched the iPad, a tablet computer that further expanded the company's product line. The iPad's large multi-touch screen, intuitive interface, and versatility made it popular for both personal and professional use. The iPad's design and functionality demonstrated Apple's ability to innovate and create new product categories.

MacBook Air

The MacBook Air, introduced in 2008, set a new standard for portable computing with its ultra-thin design and lightweight form factor. Despite its slim profile, the MacBook Air offered impressive performance and battery life, making it a favorite among professionals and travelers. Its design influenced the development of ultrabooks and other thin-and-light laptops in the industry.

The Role of Storytelling in Apple's Marketing

Steve Jobs understood the power of storytelling in marketing and used it to create compelling product narratives, deliver memorable keynote presentations, and build emotional connections with consumers. This section explores how Jobs crafted compelling product narratives, the importance of keynote presentations and product launches, and the strategies used to build emotional connections with audiences.

Crafting Compelling Product Narratives

The Art of Storytelling

Steve Jobs was a master storyteller. He knew that a compelling narrative could elevate a product from a mere piece of technology to an integral part of people's lives. Jobs crafted stories that highlighted the innovative features and benefits of Apple's products while connecting them to broader human experiences and emotions.

Highlighting the Problem

A key element of Jobs' storytelling was identifying a problem that the product aimed to solve. He framed the problem in a way that resonated with the audience, making them feel the need for a solution. By clearly articulating the problem, Jobs set the stage for introducing the product as the answer.

Introducing the Solution

After establishing the problem, Jobs introduced the product as the innovative solution. He emphasized how the product's features and design addressed the problem and improved the user's life. This approach made the product's benefits clear and relatable, enhancing its appeal.

Creating a Vision

Jobs often positioned Apple's products as part of a larger vision for the future. He painted a picture of how the product would change the way people live, work, and interact with technology. This visionary approach inspired audiences and made them feel part of something bigger.

Emotional Appeal

Jobs' narratives were rich with emotional appeal. He connected the product to universal human experiences, such as creativity, productivity, and connection. By appealing to emotions, Jobs made Apple's products more relatable and desirable.

Focus on User Stories

Jobs frequently incorporated user stories into his narratives. These stories showcased how real people used Apple products to achieve their goals and improve their lives. User stories added authenticity and demonstrated the practical value of the products. Keynote Presentations and Product Launches

Theatrical Presentation

Steve Jobs' keynote presentations were theatrical events that captivated audiences. He used dramatic elements, such as suspense and surprise, to keep the audience engaged. Jobs' ability to build anticipation and deliver unexpected reveals made his presentations memorable and impactful.

Simplicity and Clarity

Jobs' presentations were characterized by their simplicity and clarity. He used clean, minimalistic slides with large images and minimal text to convey his message. This approach ensured that the audience's attention was focused on Jobs and the product, rather than being distracted by cluttered slides.

Storytelling Structure

Jobs structured his presentations like a story, with a clear beginning, middle, and end. He started by setting the context and identifying the problem, introduced the product as the solution, and concluded with a vision for the future. This narrative structure made the presentations coherent and compelling.

Focus on Benefits

In his presentations, Jobs emphasized the benefits of the product rather than just listing its features. He explained how the product would make the user's life better, more efficient, or more enjoyable. This focus on benefits helped the audience understand the practical value of the product.

Demonstrations

Live demonstrations were a key element of Jobs' presentations. He showcased the product's features in real-time, highlighting its capabilities and ease of use. Demonstrations provided tangible evidence of the product's value and built credibility.

Use of Quotable Lines

Jobs was known for his use of memorable and quotable lines in his presentations. Phrases like "one more thing," "insanely great," and "magical" became part of the Apple lexicon and added to the excitement and anticipation surrounding the product launches.

Building Anticipation

Jobs was a master at building anticipation and excitement. He often teased upcoming products and features, creating buzz and speculation in the media and among consumers. This anticipation helped build momentum leading up to the product launch.
Building Emotional Connections

Human-Centric Marketing

Jobs' marketing approach was human-centric, focusing on how Apple products improved people's lives. By highlighting the human impact of the products, Jobs created emotional connections with consumers. This approach made the products more relatable and desirable.

Empathy and Understanding

Jobs had a deep understanding of consumer needs and desires. He empathized with their challenges and aspirations, and this empathy was reflected in Apple's marketing. By addressing these needs and desires, Jobs built a strong emotional bond with the audience.

Iconic Advertising Campaigns

Apple's advertising campaigns were known for their creativity and emotional appeal. Campaigns like "Think Different," "Get a Mac," and "Shot on iPhone" resonated with audiences by highlighting the brand's values and the human experiences associated with the products.

- Think Different: Launched in 1997, the "Think Different" campaign celebrated the "crazy ones" who changed the world. The campaign's inspirational message and iconic imagery reinforced Apple's identity as a brand that championed creativity and innovation.

- Get a Mac: The "Get a Mac" campaign, featuring the characters "Mac" and "PC," humorously highlighted the advantages of using a Mac over a PC. The campaign's relatable and entertaining approach helped build a strong emotional connection with the audience.

- Shot on iPhone: The "Shot on iPhone" campaign showcased stunning photos and videos captured by iPhone users. By celebrating the creativity of its users, the campaign reinforced the iPhone's capabilities and built a sense of community among users.

Creating a Sense of Belonging

Jobs understood the importance of creating a sense of belonging among Apple users. He positioned Apple products as tools for creativity, innovation, and self-expression, appealing to individuals who saw themselves as part of a like-minded community. This sense of belonging fostered loyalty and advocacy.

Engaging with the Community

Apple actively engaged with its community of users through events, forums, and social media. Jobs valued user feedback and incorporated it into product development and marketing. This engagement strengthened the bond between Apple and its customers.

Legacy and Impact

Jobs' ability to build emotional connections with consumers has had a lasting impact on Apple's brand and marketing strategies. His approach has influenced countless other companies and marketers, demonstrating the power of storytelling and emotional engagement in building strong brands.

Steve Jobs' approach to product design, user experience, and marketing was revolutionary. His focus on simplicity and elegance, the importance of user experience, and the creation of iconic product designs set new standards in the technology industry. Jobs' emphasis on crafting compelling product narratives, delivering memorable keynote presentations, and building emotional connections with consumers transformed Apple's marketing and established it as one of the most beloved brands in the world.

Jobs' legacy continues to influence the technology industry and marketing practices. His principles of design, user-centricity, and storytelling remain relevant and are adopted by companies seeking to create innovative and impactful products. Steve Jobs' vision, leadership, and dedication to excellence have left an indelible mark on the world, inspiring generations of entrepreneurs, designers, and marketers to think differently and strive for greatness.

Key Lessons from Apple's Most Iconic Campaigns

Apple's marketing campaigns have set benchmarks in the industry for their creativity, emotional resonance, and strategic brilliance. This section delves into three of Apple's most iconic campaigns: the "Think Different" campaign, the launches of the iPod, iPhone, and iPad, and the Apple Store experience, extracting key lessons that have contributed to Apple's enduring success.

"Think Different" Campaign

Background and Concept

Launched in 1997, the "Think Different" campaign

was a pivotal moment for Apple. At a time when the company was struggling, Steve Jobs had just returned to Apple and needed to rejuvenate its brand image and reconnect with its core audience. The campaign sought to position Apple not just as a technology company but as a brand that stood for creativity, innovation, and challenging the status quo.

Execution

The campaign featured black-and-white photographs of iconic figures who had "changed the world" by thinking differently, including Albert Einstein, Martin Luther King Jr., Mahatma Gandhi, and Pablo Picasso. The accompanying slogan, "Think Different," was a call to action and an embodiment of Apple's philosophy.

Key Lessons

- Emotional Resonance: The "Think Different" campaign tapped into deep emotional currents by celebrating human creativity and achievement. It reminded people of the potential to make a difference, aligning Apple's brand with these aspirational values.

- Brand Values: This campaign reinforced Apple's core values of innovation, creativity, and non-conformity. It communicated that Apple was not just about selling products but about empowering individuals to think creatively and challenge norms.

- Storytelling: The campaign's strength lay in its

powerful storytelling. By associating Apple with some of the greatest thinkers and innovators in history, it told a story of potential and inspiration, elevating the brand's identity.
- Simplicity: The campaign's simplicity in design—using stark, minimalist visuals and a straightforward message—ensured that the focus remained on the message and its emotional impact.

The Launch of the iPod, iPhone, and iPad

iPod

Revolutionizing Music Consumption

When the iPod was launched in 2001, it was marketed as a device that could hold "1,000 songs in your pocket." This simple yet powerful value proposition immediately resonated with consumers and set the stage for a revolution in music consumption.

Key Lessons

- Clear Value Proposition: The iPod's marketing focused on a clear and compelling value proposition. It communicated a tangible benefit that was easy to understand and highly desirable.

- Ecosystem Integration: The success of the iPod was closely tied to the iTunes ecosystem. By making it easy to purchase, organize, and transfer music, Apple created a seamless user experience that reinforced the value of the iPod.

- Lifestyle Branding: The iPod was marketed as more than just a music player; it was a lifestyle accessory. Advertising campaigns featured silhouettes of people dancing with their iPods, highlighting the product's role in enhancing everyday life.

iPhone

Transforming Communication

The iPhone, introduced in 2007, was marketed as a revolutionary device that combined a phone, an iPod, and an internet communicator. Its multi-touch interface and sleek design set it apart from any other device on the market.

Key Lessons

- Innovation Focus: The marketing of the iPhone emphasized its groundbreaking features and the ways it transformed communication and interaction. The emphasis on innovation positioned Apple as a leader in mobile technology.

- User Experience: Apple highlighted the iPhone's user-friendly interface and seamless integration with other Apple products and services. This focus on user experience created a compelling narrative that attracted a broad audience.

- Consistent Messaging: From the initial reveal to the subsequent advertising campaigns, Apple maintained consistent messaging about the iPhone's capabilities and benefits. This consistency helped reinforce the product's value proposition.

iPad

Creating a New Category

The iPad, launched in 2010, was introduced as a device that fit between a smartphone and a laptop. Its marketing emphasized its versatility for work, play, and everything in between.

Key Lessons

- Category Creation: Apple successfully created a new product category with the iPad. The marketing campaigns clearly articulated its use cases, making it easy for consumers to understand where the iPad fit in their lives.

- Demonstrations: Apple used live demonstrations to showcase the iPad's capabilities. These demonstrations highlighted the product's versatility and ease of use, making a strong case for its value.

- Visual Appeal: The marketing for the iPad emphasized its sleek design and high-quality display, reinforcing Apple's reputation for superior aesthetics and craftsmanship.

The Apple Store Experience

Revolutionizing Retail

The opening of the first Apple Store in 2001 marked a new era in retail. Apple Stores were designed to offer more than just a place to buy products; they were meant to provide an immersive brand experience.

Key Lessons

- Experience Over Sales: Apple Stores were designed to provide a unique customer experience. The emphasis was on allowing customers to interact with products and receive personalized support, rather than just making a sale.

- Innovative Design: The stores featured minimalist designs, open spaces, and hands-on product displays. This design philosophy created a welcoming and engaging environment that encouraged exploration.

- Genius Bar: The introduction of the Genius Bar provided customers with access to expert support and advice. This focus on customer service helped build trust and loyalty.

- Community Engagement: Apple Stores became community hubs where customers could attend workshops, product launches, and other events. This community engagement reinforced Apple's brand values and created a loyal customer base.

The Importance of Vision and Leadership in Branding

Steve Jobs' vision and leadership were instrumental in shaping Apple's brand and driving its success. His leadership style, focus on building a visionary brand, and ability to inspire and motivate teams set Apple apart from its competitors. This section explores Jobs' leadership style, the importance of building a visionary brand, and strategies for inspiring and motivating teams.

Jobs' Leadership Style

Visionary Leadership

Steve Jobs was a visionary leader with a clear and compelling vision for Apple's future. He was able to see the potential of technology to change the world and communicated this vision passionately. Jobs' ability to articulate a clear vision inspired his team and drove Apple's innovation.

Attention to Detail

Jobs' meticulous attention to detail was a defining aspect of his leadership style. He was involved in every aspect of product development, from design to functionality. This attention to detail ensured that Apple's products met the highest standards of quality and user experience.

Bold Decision-Making

Jobs was known for his bold decision-making and

willingness to take risks. He was not afraid to make unpopular decisions if he believed they were in the best interest of the company. This boldness allowed Apple to innovate and stay ahead of the competition.

Focus on Innovation

Innovation was at the core of Jobs' leadership. He encouraged his team to think creatively and push the boundaries of what was possible. This focus on innovation led to the development of groundbreaking products that transformed entire industries.

Demanding Excellence

Jobs had high expectations and demanded excellence from his team. He believed in the importance of hard work and dedication, and his drive for perfection pushed his team to achieve remarkable results.

Empowering Teams

Despite his demanding nature, Jobs also empowered his teams by giving them the autonomy to experiment and innovate. He trusted his team members to deliver exceptional work and provided them with the resources and support they needed to succeed.

Building a Visionary Brand

Articulating a Clear Vision

A clear and compelling vision is essential for building a visionary brand. Jobs' vision for Apple was not just about creating products but about making a meaningful impact on the world. This vision resonated with both employees and customers, creating a strong sense of purpose and direction.

Aligning Brand Values

Apple's brand values of innovation, creativity, and quality were consistently reflected in its products, marketing, and customer experiences. Aligning brand values with the company's vision ensured that every aspect of the brand reinforced its identity.

Consistency in Messaging

Consistent messaging is crucial for building a strong brand. Apple's marketing campaigns, product launches, and customer interactions all conveyed a consistent message about the brand's values and vision. This consistency helped build trust and loyalty among customers.

Creating Iconic Products

Apple's iconic products, such as the iPod, iPhone, and MacBook, became symbols of the brand's innovation and quality. These products not only met customer needs but also exceeded their expectations, reinforcing Apple's reputation as a visionary brand.

Emotional Connection

Jobs understood the importance of creating an emotional connection with customers. Apple's products and marketing campaigns were designed to resonate with customers on an emotional level, creating a sense of loyalty and attachment to the brand.

Customer-Centric Approach

A customer-centric approach was central to Apple's brand strategy. Jobs believed in understanding and anticipating customer needs and designing products that delivered exceptional user experiences. This focus on the customer helped build a loyal and engaged customer base.

Inspiring and Motivating Teams

Communicating the Vision

Communicating a clear and inspiring vision is essential for motivating teams. Jobs was able to articulate his vision for Apple in a way that inspired his team and made them feel part of something significant. This shared vision created a sense of purpose and motivation.

Fostering a Culture of Innovation

Jobs fostered a culture of innovation by encouraging his team to think creatively and take risks. He provided an environment where experimentation was valued, and failures were seen as opportunities to learn and improve. This culture of innovation drove Apple's success and kept the company at the forefront of the industry.

Recognizing and Rewarding Excellence

Recognizing and rewarding excellence is crucial for motivating teams. Jobs acknowledged the hard work and achievements of his team members, reinforcing their commitment to excellence. This recognition created a positive and motivating work environment.

Providing Autonomy and Responsibility

Jobs empowered his team by giving them the autonomy to make decisions and take ownership of their work. He trusted his team members to deliver exceptional results and provided them with the responsibility and resources they needed to succeed.

Encouraging Collaboration

Collaboration was a key aspect of Jobs' leadership style. He believed that the best ideas often emerged from collaborative efforts and encouraged his team to work together and share their insights. This collaborative approach fostered creativity and innovation.

Leading by Example

Jobs led by example, demonstrating his commitment to the company's vision and values. His passion, dedication, and attention to detail set a standard for his team and inspired them to strive for excellence.

Creating a Sense of Belonging

Jobs created a sense of belonging within his team by

fostering a strong company culture and a shared sense of purpose. He made his team members feel valued and appreciated, creating a positive and motivating work environment.

Steve Jobs' approach to product design, user experience, marketing, and leadership played a crucial role in Apple's success and enduring legacy. His focus on simplicity, elegance, and user-centric design set new standards in the technology industry. Jobs' ability to craft compelling product narratives, deliver memorable keynote presentations, and build emotional connections with consumers transformed Apple's marketing and established it as one of the most beloved brands in the world.

The key lessons from Apple's most iconic campaigns, including the "Think Different" campaign, the launches of the iPod, iPhone, and iPad, and the Apple Store experience, highlight the importance of emotional resonance, clear value propositions, and exceptional customer experiences. Jobs' visionary leadership, attention to detail, and focus on innovation and excellence inspired and motivated his teams to achieve remarkable results.

Steve Jobs' legacy continues to influence the technology industry and marketing practices. His principles of design, user-centricity, storytelling, and leadership remain relevant and are adopted by companies seeking to create innovative and impactful products. Steve Jobs' vision, leadership, and dedication to excellence have left an indelible mark on the world, inspiring generations of entrepreneurs, designers, and marketers to think differently and strive for greatness.

Chapter 7

Gary Vaynerchuk Social Media and Digital Marketing

Gary Vaynerchuk, a name synonymous with social media and digital marketing, has become one of the most influential voices in the industry. Known for his energetic personality, business acumen, and forward-thinking approach to marketing, Vaynerchuk's journey from a family-run liquor store to founding VaynerMedia is a testament to his relentless drive and innovative mindset. This section explores his early life and family business, his rise through Wine Library TV, and the founding of VaynerMedia.

Early Life

Gary Vaynerchuk was born on November 14, 1975, in Babruysk, Belarus, then part of the Soviet Union. His family immigrated to the United States when he was three years old, settling in Edison, New Jersey. From a young age, Vaynerchuk displayed an entrepreneurial spirit, starting various small businesses such as lemonade stands and selling baseball cards.

Family Business

In 1983, Vaynerchuk's father, Sasha, purchased a local

liquor store in Springfield, New Jersey, called Shopper's Discount Liquors. Gary began working at the store at the age of 14, stocking shelves and bagging ice. It was here that he developed a passion for the wine industry and learned valuable lessons about customer service and retail operations.

After graduating from Mount Ida College in Newton, Massachusetts, Vaynerchuk returned to the family business with a vision to transform it. He saw the potential to leverage the internet to expand the business and reach a wider audience.

Rise through Wine Library TV

Transformation of the Family Business

In 1997, Vaynerchuk convinced his father to change the name of the store to Wine Library and launched WineLibrary.com, one of the first e-commerce platforms for wine. His efforts to bring the business online were instrumental in increasing sales, and he quickly grew the company's revenue from $3 million to $60 million annually.

Wine Library TV

In 2006, Vaynerchuk launched Wine Library TV, a daily video blog where he reviewed wines and shared his knowledge and enthusiasm for the industry. Unlike traditional wine critics, Vaynerchuk's approach was informal, energetic, and accessible, appealing to a younger audience and demystifying the world of wine.

Innovative Marketing Techniques

Wine Library TV was revolutionary for its time, leveraging the emerging platform of YouTube to reach a global audience. Vaynerchuk's authenticity, passion, and engaging personality resonated with viewers, and the show quickly gained a loyal following. He used social media platforms like Twitter and Facebook to promote the show and engage with his audience, pioneering many of the digital marketing techniques that are now commonplace.

Building a Personal Brand

Through Wine Library TV, Vaynerchuk not only promoted the family business but also built his personal brand. He became known as an expert in the wine industry and a savvy marketer who understood the power of social media. His success with Wine Library TV showcased his ability to adapt to new technologies and leverage them to create significant business growth.

Founding VaynerMedia

Identifying a New Opportunity

As Vaynerchuk's profile grew, he recognized the potential to help other businesses leverage social media and digital marketing. In 2009, he co-founded VaynerMedia with his younger brother, AJ Vaynerchuk. The company was established with the goal of providing full-service digital marketing and social media strategy to large corporations and Fortune 500 companies.

Growth and Expansion

VaynerMedia quickly gained traction, thanks to Gary's reputation and expertise. The agency focused on helping brands navigate the rapidly changing digital landscape, creating content and strategies tailored to each platform. Vaynerchuk's emphasis on storytelling, authenticity, and engaging with audiences in meaningful ways set VaynerMedia apart from traditional marketing agencies.

The company expanded its services to include influencer marketing, media buying, content creation, and more. Under Gary's leadership, VaynerMedia grew rapidly, attracting high-profile clients such as PepsiCo, GE, Johnson & Johnson, and Chase.

Innovative Campaigns

VaynerMedia became known for its innovative and effective campaigns, which often went viral and garnered significant media attention. The agency's ability to create culturally relevant content and leverage the power of social media influencers made it a leader in the industry.

VaynerX and Diversification

In addition to VaynerMedia, Vaynerchuk launched VaynerX, a modern media and communications holding company that encompasses various businesses, including Gallery Media Group, VaynerSpeakers, and Tracer, a SaaS product for marketing analytics. This diversification allowed Vaynerchuk to expand his influence and provide a broader range of services to clients.

VaynerSports and Other Ventures

Vaynerchuk also ventured into sports representation with the founding of VaynerSports, an agency representing athletes in the NFL, MLB, and other sports. This move was in line with his belief in the power of personal branding and his commitment to helping individuals maximize their potential.

Educational Initiatives

Recognizing the need to educate the next generation of marketers and entrepreneurs, Vaynerchuk launched various educational initiatives, including VaynerX's 4Ds (Daily Digital Deep Dive) program, which offers immersive workshops on digital marketing. He also wrote several best-selling books, such as "Crush It!," "Jab, Jab, Jab, Right Hook," and "The Thank You Economy," sharing his insights and strategies with a wider audience.

Impact on the Industry

Gary Vaynerchuk's rise to prominence through Wine Library TV and the founding of VaynerMedia has had a profound impact on the marketing industry. He has been a pioneer in recognizing the potential of social media and digital marketing, advocating for their use long before they became mainstream. His innovative strategies and emphasis on authenticity and storytelling have influenced countless marketers and businesses.

Emphasis on Personal Branding

One of Vaynerchuk's key contributions to the industry is his emphasis on personal branding. He has demonstrated that individuals can leverage social media to build their brands and create opportunities. By sharing his journey and insights, he has inspired many to take control of their personal and professional narratives.

Advocacy for New Platforms

Vaynerchuk has consistently been at the forefront of adopting and advocating for new platforms and technologies. He was an early adopter of platforms like YouTube, Twitter, and Instagram, and has since championed newer platforms like TikTok and LinkedIn. His ability to recognize and capitalize on emerging trends has kept him relevant and influential in the ever-changing digital landscape.

Focus on Authenticity and Engagement

Vaynerchuk's approach to marketing emphasizes authenticity and genuine engagement with audiences. He advocates for building real relationships and providing value, rather than just focusing on sales. This philosophy has resonated with many and has helped shift the industry towards more customer-centric and ethical practices.

Educational Contributions

Through his books, speaking engagements, and online content, Vaynerchuk has made significant educational contributions to the marketing community. He shares practical advice, insights, and strategies that empower individuals and businesses to succeed in the digital age.

Legacy and Influence

Gary Vaynerchuk's legacy in the social media and digital marketing industry is marked by his innovative spirit, commitment to authenticity, and dedication to helping others succeed. He has built a multifaceted career that spans entrepreneurship, marketing, education, and media. His influence continues to grow as he explores new ventures and shares his knowledge with a global audience.

Gary Vaynerchuk's journey from a family-run liquor store to becoming a leading voice in social media and digital marketing is a remarkable story of vision, innovation, and relentless drive. Through his work with Wine Library TV, VaynerMedia, and various other ventures, Vaynerchuk has demonstrated the power of leveraging digital platforms to build brands, engage with audiences, and drive business growth.

His emphasis on personal branding, authenticity, and engagement has reshaped the marketing landscape, inspiring countless individuals and businesses to embrace new technologies and strategies. Vaynerchuk's impact extends beyond his entrepreneurial achievements, as he continues to educate, motivate, and influence the next generation of marketers and entrepreneurs.

Gary Vaynerchuk's biography and rise to prominence

serve as a powerful example of how embracing change, staying ahead of trends, and prioritizing genuine connections can lead to extraordinary success in the digital age. His contributions to the industry will continue to shape the future of marketing and inspire those who seek to make their mark in the world.

The Power of Social Media in Modern Marketing

Social media has become a cornerstone of modern marketing, offering unparalleled opportunities for brands to engage with audiences, build communities, and measure success. This section explores the various platforms and strategies used in social media marketing, the methods for engaging with audiences, and the tools and metrics for measuring success. Platforms and Strategies

Major Social Media Platforms

- Facebook: With over 2.8 billion monthly active users, Facebook remains a dominant platform for social media marketing. It offers a wide range of advertising options, including targeted ads, sponsored posts, and video ads. Facebook's robust analytics tools allow marketers to track the performance of their campaigns and optimize their strategies.

- Instagram: Owned by Facebook, Instagram is a visual-centric platform with over 1 billion monthly active users. It is particularly popular among younger demographics. Instagram's features, such as Stories, IGTV, and Shopping, provide diverse opportunities for brands to showcase their products and engage with followers through visually appealing content.

- Twitter: Known for its real-time updates and concise messaging, Twitter has over 330 million monthly active users. It is an ideal platform for brands to engage in conversations, provide customer service, and share news and updates. Twitter's advertising options include promoted tweets, trends, and accounts.

- LinkedIn: With over 740 million members, LinkedIn is the go-to platform for B2B marketing and professional networking. Brands can leverage LinkedIn to share industry insights, publish articles, and connect with potential clients and partners. LinkedIn Ads offers targeted advertising options based on job titles, industries, and company sizes.

- TikTok: TikTok has rapidly gained popularity, especially among Gen Z, with over 1 billion monthly active users. The platform's short-form video content allows brands to create engaging and entertaining videos that resonate with younger audiences. TikTok's advertising options include in-feed ads, branded hashtags, and sponsored challenges.

- YouTube: As the second-largest search engine in the world, YouTube boasts over 2 billion monthly active users. Brands can leverage YouTube to create long-form video content, tutorials, product reviews, and more. YouTube Ads provides various advertising options, including pre-roll ads, display ads, and sponsored content.

- Strategies for Social Media Marketing

- Content Marketing: Creating and sharing valuable content that educates, entertains, or inspires the audience. This can include blog posts, videos, infographics, and user-generated content. Content marketing helps establish the brand as an authority in its industry and drives organic engagement.

- Influencer Marketing: Collaborating with influencers who have a significant following and influence over the target audience. Influencer marketing can increase brand awareness, credibility, and reach. It is essential to choose influencers whose values and audience align with the brand.

- Social Media Advertising: Running paid campaigns to reach a broader audience. Social media platforms offer advanced targeting options based on demographics, interests, behaviors, and location. Paid advertising can drive traffic, generate leads, and increase conversions.

- Community Building: Creating and nurturing a community around the brand. This involves engaging with followers, responding to comments and messages, and encouraging user-generated content. Building a community fosters loyalty and advocacy.

- Real-Time Marketing: Capitalizing on current events, trends, and conversations to create timely and relevant content. Real-time marketing helps brands stay relevant and engage with the audience in a meaningful way.

- Analytics and Optimization: Using analytics tools to track the performance of social media campaigns. Metrics such as reach, engagement, click-through rates, and conversions provide insights into what works and what doesn't. Continuous optimization ensures that strategies remain effective and aligned with business goals.

Engaging with Audiences

Understanding the Audience

- Audience Research: Conducting research to understand the target audience's demographics, interests, behaviors, and preferences. Tools such as social media analytics, surveys, and customer feedback help gather valuable insights.

- Creating Personas: Developing detailed personas that represent different segments of the target audience. Personas help marketers tailor their content and messaging to resonate with specific audience groups.

- Content Creation

- Relevant and Valuable Content: Creating content that addresses the audience's needs, interests, and pain points. Valuable content can include how-to guides, educational articles, entertaining videos, and inspirational stories.

- Visual Appeal: Using high-quality images, videos, and graphics to capture the audience's attention. Visual content is more engaging and shareable than text-only content.

- Storytelling: Crafting compelling stories that connect with the audience on an emotional level. Storytelling helps humanize the brand and make it more relatable.

Engagement Techniques

- Interactive Content: Creating interactive content such as polls, quizzes, contests, and live videos to encourage audience participation. Interactive content boosts engagement and provides valuable insights into audience preferences.

- Personalization: Personalizing content and interactions based on the audience's preferences and behaviors. Personalization can include personalized messages, product recommendations, and targeted ads.

- User-Generated Content: Encouraging followers to create and share content related to the brand. User-generated content builds authenticity and trust, and it can be repurposed for marketing campaigns.

- Community Management: Actively managing the brand's social media communities by responding to comments, messages, and reviews. Community management fosters a positive brand image and strengthens relationships with followers.

- Influencer Collaborations: Partnering with influencers to co-create content and engage with their followers. Influencers can amplify the brand's reach and credibility.

Measuring Success

Key Metrics

- Reach and Impressions: Measuring the number of unique users who see the brand's content (reach) and the total number of times the content is displayed (impressions). High reach and impressions indicate strong brand visibility.

- Engagement: Tracking likes, comments, shares, and reactions to gauge audience interaction with the content. High engagement rates indicate that the content resonates with the audience.

- Click-Through Rate (CTR): Measuring the percentage of users who click on a link or call-to-action in the content. A high CTR indicates that the content effectively drives traffic to the brand's website or landing page.

- Conversions: Tracking the number of users who complete a desired action, such as making a purchase, signing up for a newsletter, or downloading an e-book. Conversions measure the effectiveness of social media campaigns in driving business outcomes.

- Return on Investment (ROI): Calculating the return on investment for social media campaigns by comparing the revenue generated to the costs incurred. Positive ROI indicates that the campaigns are cost-effective and contribute to business growth.

- Sentiment Analysis: Analyzing the sentiment of mentions, comments, and reviews to understand how the audience perceives the brand. Positive sentiment indicates a strong brand reputation, while negative sentiment highlights areas for improvement.

Tools for Measurement

- Native Analytics: Using built-in analytics tools provided by social media platforms, such as Facebook Insights, Instagram Insights, Twitter Analytics, and LinkedIn Analytics. These tools offer detailed metrics on reach, engagement, and audience demographics.

- Third-Party Tools: Utilizing third-party

analytics tools such as Hootsuite, Sprout Social, Buffer, and Google Analytics. These tools provide comprehensive analytics and reporting features, allowing marketers to track performance across multiple platforms.

- Social Listening Tools: Using social listening tools like Brandwatch, Mention, and Sprinklr to monitor brand mentions, track trends, and analyze sentiment. Social listening helps brands stay informed about audience opinions and industry trends.

Content Creation and Personal Branding Strategies

Content creation and personal branding are essential components of modern marketing. By creating valuable content and building a strong personal brand, individuals and businesses can establish themselves as thought leaders, attract loyal followers, and drive business growth. This section explores strategies for creating valuable content, building a personal brand, and provides examples of effective personal branding.

Creating Valuable Content

Understanding the Audience

- Audience Research: Conducting thorough research to understand the target audience's interests, needs, and preferences. Tools such as surveys, social media analytics, and audience feedback provide valuable insights.

- Content Personas: Developing content personas that represent different segments of the audience. Personas help tailor content to meet the specific needs and interests of each group.

Content Planning

- Content Calendar: Creating a content calendar to plan and schedule content in advance. A content calendar ensures consistency and helps maintain a steady flow of content.

- Content Mix: Balancing different types of content, such as educational, entertaining, inspirational, and promotional. A diverse content mix keeps the audience engaged and caters to various interests.

- Content Themes: Establishing content themes that align with the brand's values and resonate with the audience. Themes provide a cohesive framework for content creation.

Content Creation

- High-Quality Content: Prioritizing quality over quantity. High-quality content is well-researched, well-written, and visually appealing. It provides value to the audience and reflects positively on the brand.

- Visual Content: Incorporating images, videos, infographics, and other visual elements to enhance the appeal and shareability of the content. Visual content captures attention and improves engagement.

- Storytelling: Using storytelling techniques to create compelling narratives that connect with the audience on an emotional level. Stories humanize the brand and make it more relatable.

- Originality: Creating original content that offers unique perspectives and insights. Original content differentiates the brand and establishes it as a thought leader.

Content Distribution

- Social Media: Sharing content on social media platforms to reach a broader audience. Tailoring content to fit the format and audience of each platform.

- Email Marketing: Distributing content through email newsletters to keep the audience informed and engaged. Email marketing allows for personalized content delivery.

- Blogging: Publishing content on a blog to drive organic traffic and improve SEO. Blogging provides a platform for in-depth content and thought leadership.

- Collaborations: Collaborating with influencers, industry experts, and other brands to co-create and share content. Collaborations expand reach and enhance credibility.

Building a Personal Brand

Defining the Personal Brand

- **Brand Identity:** Defining the core values, mission, and unique selling proposition of the personal brand. A clear brand identity guides all branding efforts.

- **Brand Voice:** Establishing a consistent brand voice that reflects the personality and values of the individual. The brand voice should be authentic and resonate with the target audience.

- **Brand Story:** Crafting a compelling brand story that highlights the individual's journey, achievements, and vision. The brand story humanizes the brand and creates an emotional connection with the audience.

Building an Online Presence

- **Website:** Creating a professional website that serves as the central hub for the personal brand. The website should include an about page, portfolio, blog, and contact information.

- **Social Media Profiles:** Setting up and optimizing social media profiles on platforms relevant to the target audience. Consistent branding across profiles reinforces the brand identity.

- **Content Creation:** Regularly creating and

sharing valuable content that aligns with the personal brand. Content should showcase expertise, provide value, and engage the audience.

Networking and Engagement

- Online Communities: Joining and participating in online communities and forums related to the industry. Engaging with peers and industry experts helps build credibility and expand the network.

- Networking Events: Attending industry conferences, workshops, and networking events to connect with potential clients, collaborators, and mentors. Building relationships offline enhances the personal brand.

- Engagement: Actively engaging with the audience by responding to comments, messages, and feedback. Engaging with the audience fosters loyalty and strengthens relationships.

Leveraging Media and Public Relations

- Guest Blogging: Writing guest posts for reputable blogs and publications to reach a wider audience and establish authority.

- Media Appearances: Seeking opportunities for media appearances, such as interviews, podcasts, and speaking engagements. Media exposure enhances visibility and credibility.

- Public Relations: Building relationships with journalists and media outlets to secure press coverage and features. Positive media coverage boosts the personal brand's reputation.

Examples of Effective Personal Branding

Gary Vaynerchuk

Gary Vaynerchuk is a prime example of effective personal branding. He built his personal brand through authentic content, consistent engagement, and a clear value proposition. Vaynerchuk shares his journey, insights, and advice through various channels, including social media, books, podcasts, and speaking engagements. His personal brand is synonymous with entrepreneurship, digital marketing, and hustle, attracting a loyal following of aspiring entrepreneurs and marketers.

Marie Forleo

Marie Forleo is a successful entrepreneur, author, and motivational speaker known for her personal brand centered around business and personal development. She built her brand through her online show, MarieTV, where she shares valuable advice and interviews industry experts. Forleo's authenticity, positivity, and practical insights have garnered a dedicated audience. Her brand emphasizes empowerment, creativity, and the belief that "everything is figureoutable."

Neil Patel

Neil Patel is a renowned digital marketer and co-founder of several successful companies, including Crazy Egg and Kissmetrics. He built his personal brand by sharing his expertise through blog posts, podcasts, videos, and speaking engagements. Patel's actionable advice and in-depth knowledge of SEO and digital marketing have established him as a thought leader in the industry. His personal brand is characterized by transparency, credibility, and a commitment to helping businesses grow.

Brené Brown

Brené Brown is a research professor, author, and speaker known for her work on vulnerability, courage, and empathy. She built her personal brand through TED Talks, books, and public speaking engagements. Brown's relatable storytelling, research-based insights, and focus on human connection have resonated with a global audience. Her personal brand emphasizes authenticity, resilience, and the power of vulnerability.

Tony Robbins

Tony Robbins is a world-renowned life coach, author, and motivational speaker known for his dynamic speaking style and transformative programs. He built his personal brand through live events, seminars, books, and media appearances. Robbins' high energy presentations, practical advice, and commitment to personal growth have earned him a massive following. His personal brand is associated with empowerment, success, and peak performance.

The power of social media in modern marketing cannot be overstated. Social media platforms provide brands with the tools and opportunities to engage with audiences, build communities, and measure success. Effective social media strategies include content marketing, influencer marketing, social media advertising, community building, real-time marketing, and continuous optimization. Engaging with audiences requires understanding their needs, creating valuable content, and fostering meaningful interactions.

Content creation and personal branding are essential for establishing authority, attracting followers, and driving business growth. Creating valuable content involves understanding the audience, planning strategically, and leveraging visual appeal and storytelling. Building a personal brand requires defining a clear brand identity, building an online presence, networking, and leveraging media opportunities. Examples of successful personal branding demonstrate the importance of authenticity, consistency, and providing value to the audience.

By embracing social media, content creation, and personal branding strategies, individuals and businesses can thrive in the digital age, build strong relationships with their audience, and achieve long-term success.

Engaging with Audiences and Building a Community

Engaging with audiences and building a community are essential components of modern marketing. By fostering interaction and creating a sense of belonging, brands can cultivate loyalty, drive engagement, and build a supportive community. This section explores interaction and engagement techniques, community-building strategies, and case studies of successful engagement.
Interaction and Engagement Techniques

Understanding the Audience

- Audience Research: Conduct thorough research to understand the demographics, interests, and preferences of your target audience. Use tools like surveys, social media analytics, and customer feedback to gather valuable insights.

- Creating Personas: Develop detailed personas that represent different segments of your audience. These personas help tailor your content and engagement strategies to meet the specific needs and interests of each group.

Content Creation

- High-Quality Content: Focus on creating high-quality content that provides value to your audience. This can include educational articles, entertaining videos, inspirational stories, and how-to guides. High-quality content helps

build trust and credibility.
- Visual Content: Incorporate images, videos, infographics, and other visual elements to enhance the appeal and shareability of your content. Visual content is more engaging and can capture the audience's attention more effectively.

- Storytelling: Use storytelling techniques to create compelling narratives that connect with your audience on an emotional level. Stories humanize your brand and make it more relatable.

Interactive Content

- Polls and Quizzes: Create polls and quizzes to encourage audience participation and gather insights. Interactive content boosts engagement and provides valuable data on audience preferences.

- Contests and Giveaways: Run contests and giveaways to incentivize participation and reward your audience. These activities can increase brand visibility and attract new followers.

- Live Videos: Host live videos, such as Q&A sessions, product demonstrations, and behind-the-scenes content, to interact with your audience in real-time. Live videos create a sense of immediacy and foster a deeper connection.

Personalization

- Tailored Content: Personalize your content based on audience preferences and behaviors. Use data and analytics to deliver personalized recommendations, messages, and offers.

- Segmentation: Segment your audience based on demographics, interests, and behaviors to deliver more relevant and targeted content. Segmentation helps increase the effectiveness of your engagement efforts.

Community Management

- Responding to Comments and Messages: Actively engage with your audience by responding to comments, messages, and reviews. Prompt and thoughtful responses demonstrate that you value your audience's input and foster a positive brand image.

- Encouraging User-Generated Content: Encourage your audience to create and share content related to your brand. User-generated content builds authenticity and trust and can be repurposed for marketing campaigns.

- Creating a Safe and Inclusive Environment: Foster a safe and inclusive environment where all audience members feel welcome and valued. Establish clear community guidelines and address any negative behavior promptly.

Community-Building Strategies

Creating a Sense of Belonging

- Shared Values and Purpose: Communicate your brand's values and purpose clearly to resonate with your audience. A shared sense of purpose fosters a sense of belonging and loyalty.

- Community Identity: Develop a strong community identity by using consistent branding, messaging, and visuals. This identity helps create a cohesive and recognizable community.

Building Trust and Credibility

- Transparency: Be transparent about your brand's practices, policies, and values. Transparency builds trust and credibility with your audience.

- Consistency: Maintain consistency in your content, messaging, and interactions. Consistency reinforces your brand's identity and helps build a loyal community.

Encouraging Participation

- Member Contributions: Encourage community members to contribute their ideas, opinions, and content. Highlight and celebrate these contributions to show appreciation and foster a sense of ownership.

- Interactive Activities: Organize interactive activities, such as discussions, challenges, and events, to encourage participation and engagement. These activities help strengthen the community bond.

Providing Value

- Exclusive Content: Offer exclusive content, such as behind-the-scenes access, early product releases, and special offers, to your community members. Exclusive content provides added value and rewards loyalty.

- Educational Resources: Provide educational resources, such as webinars, workshops, and tutorials, to help your community members learn and grow. Educational content enhances the value of being part of the community.

Fostering Relationships

- Community Engagement: Actively engage with your community through regular interactions, updates, and feedback. Building strong relationships with your community members fosters loyalty and advocacy.

- Networking Opportunities: Create opportunities for community members to connect and network with each other. Networking strengthens the community and enhances the sense of belonging.

Case Studies of Successful Engagement

1. Glossier

Background:

Glossier, a beauty brand, has successfully built a loyal community by engaging with its audience through social media and user-generated content.

Strategies:

- User-Generated Content: Glossier encourages customers to share their experiences and product reviews on social media using branded hashtags. The brand frequently features user-generated content on its own channels, creating a sense of community and authenticity.

- Customer Feedback: Glossier actively seeks and incorporates customer feedback into its product development process. This involvement makes customers feel valued and invested in the brand.

- Engaging Content: The brand shares relatable and engaging content, including tutorials, behind-the-scenes videos, and customer stories, to connect with its audience on a personal level.

Results:

Glossier's community-driven approach has resulted in

a highly engaged and loyal customer base. The brand's emphasis on authenticity and customer involvement has helped it stand out in the competitive beauty industry.

2. Peloton

Background:

Peloton, a fitness company, has created a strong community of fitness enthusiasts through its interactive and engaging platform.

Strategies:

- Live and On-Demand Classes: Peloton offers live and on-demand fitness classes that allow members to interact with instructors and fellow participants in real-time. This interactivity fosters a sense of community and motivation.

- Leaderboards and Challenges: The platform features leaderboards and challenges that encourage friendly competition and participation. These features create a sense of camaraderie and drive engagement.

- Community Groups: Peloton has established community groups on social media where members can connect, share their progress, and support each other. These groups enhance the sense of belonging and community.

Results:

Peloton's interactive and community-focused approach has resulted in a dedicated and passionate user base. The brand's emphasis on engagement and community has contributed to its rapid growth and success.

3. LEGO

Background:

LEGO, a global toy company, has built a thriving community of fans and enthusiasts through its interactive and creative initiatives.
Strategies:

- LEGO Ideas: LEGO Ideas is a platform where fans can submit their own LEGO set designs. The community votes on submissions, and winning designs are produced as official LEGO sets. This initiative empowers fans and fosters creativity.

- Social Media Engagement: LEGO actively engages with its audience on social media by sharing user-generated content, hosting contests, and responding to comments. This engagement builds a strong connection with fans.

- Events and Workshops: LEGO organizes events, workshops, and competitions that bring the community together and celebrate creativity. These activities enhance the sense of community and belonging.

Results:

LEGO's community-driven approach has resulted in a highly engaged and loyal fan base. The brand's emphasis on creativity and interaction has helped it maintain its position as a leader in the toy industry. Tips for Leveraging Digital Platforms to Grow a Brand

Leveraging digital platforms effectively is essential for growing a brand in today's competitive landscape. This section provides tips on utilizing various social media platforms, the differences between paid and organic strategies, and future trends in digital marketing.

Utilizing Various Social Media Platforms

Understanding Each Platform

- Facebook: Ideal for building a community and sharing a variety of content, including articles, videos, and live streams. Use Facebook Groups to create exclusive communities and engage with members.

- Instagram: Perfect for visual storytelling and brand aesthetics. Utilize features like Stories, IGTV, and Shopping to showcase products and connect with followers.

- Twitter: Great for real-time updates, customer service, and engaging in conversations. Use Twitter to share news, respond to queries, and participate in trending topics.

- LinkedIn: Best for B2B marketing and professional networking. Share industry insights, publish articles, and connect with potential clients and partners on LinkedIn.

- TikTok: Ideal for short-form, creative video content. Use TikTok to engage with younger audiences through entertaining and viral content.

- YouTube: Perfect for long-form video content, tutorials, and product reviews. Create a YouTube channel to share valuable video content and build a subscriber base.

Content Tailoring

- Platform-Specific Content: Tailor your content to fit the format and audience of each platform. For example, use visually appealing images and videos on Instagram, share in-depth articles on LinkedIn, and create engaging short videos on TikTok.

- Consistency: Maintain a consistent posting schedule to keep your audience engaged and informed. Consistency helps build trust and reinforces your brand presence.

Cross-Promotion

- Integrated Campaigns: Create integrated marketing campaigns that leverage multiple platforms to reach a broader audience. Use consistent messaging and visuals across platforms for a cohesive brand experience.

- Cross-Promoting Content: Share content across different platforms to maximize reach. For example, promote your YouTube videos on Facebook and Instagram, and share blog posts on LinkedIn and Twitter.

Paid vs. Organic Strategies

Organic Strategies

- Content Marketing: Focus on creating valuable and engaging content that attracts and retains your audience. Organic content marketing builds trust and credibility over time.

- SEO: Optimize your content for search engines to increase visibility and drive organic traffic. Use relevant keywords, meta tags, and high-quality backlinks to improve your SEO.

- Engagement: Actively engage with your audience by responding to comments, messages, and reviews. Engagement fosters relationships and builds a loyal community.

Paid Strategies

- Targeted Advertising: Use paid advertising to reach specific audience segments based on demographics, interests, and behaviors. Platforms like Facebook, Instagram, and

LinkedIn offer advanced targeting options.

- **Retargeting:** Implement retargeting campaigns to reach users who have previously interacted with your brand. Retargeting helps re-engage potential customers and drive conversions.

- **Influencer Partnerships:** Collaborate with influencers to promote your brand to their followers. Paid influencer partnerships can increase brand awareness and credibility.

Balancing Paid and Organic

- **Integrated Approach:** Combine paid and organic strategies for a holistic marketing approach. Use paid ads to amplify your organic content and reach a wider audience.

- **Measuring ROI:** Track the performance of both paid and organic campaigns to measure ROI and adjust your strategies accordingly. Use analytics tools to gather insights and optimize your efforts.

Future Trends in Digital Marketing

AI and Automation

- **Personalization:** Use AI and automation to deliver personalized content and experiences to your audience. Personalization enhances engagement and drives conversions.

- **Chatbots:** Implement chatbots for customer

service and support. Chatbots provide instant responses and improve customer satisfaction.

Video Marketing

- Live Streaming: Leverage live streaming to connect with your audience in real-time. Live streaming fosters authenticity and immediate engagement.

- Short-Form Videos: Create short-form videos for platforms like TikTok and Instagram Reels. Short-form videos are highly engaging and shareable.

Voice Search Optimization

- Voice Search SEO: Optimize your content for voice search by using natural language and long-tail keywords. Voice search is becoming increasingly popular with the rise of smart speakers.

- Voice Assistants: Integrate voice assistants into your digital strategy to provide a seamless user experience. Voice assistants can enhance customer interactions and accessibility.

Social Commerce

- Shoppable Posts: Utilize shoppable posts on platforms like Instagram and Facebook to enable direct purchases from social media. Social commerce streamlines the buying process.

- Livestream Shopping: Explore livestream shopping to showcase products and interact with customers in real-time. Livestream shopping combines entertainment with e-commerce.

Augmented Reality (AR)

- AR Experiences: Create AR experiences that allow customers to visualize products in their environment. AR enhances the shopping experience and reduces purchase uncertainty.

- AR Filters: Use AR filters on platforms like Snapchat and Instagram to engage users and promote your brand in a fun and interactive way.

Engaging with audiences and building a community are essential for modern marketing success. By using interaction and engagement techniques, creating valuable content, and fostering a sense of belonging, brands can cultivate loyal and supportive communities. Successful case studies, such as Glossier, Peloton, and LEGO, demonstrate the power of community-driven strategies in building strong brand connections.

Leveraging digital platforms effectively requires understanding each platform, tailoring content, and balancing paid and organic strategies. As digital marketing continues to evolve, staying ahead of trends such as AI and automation, video marketing, voice search optimization, social commerce, and augmented reality will be crucial for maintaining a competitive edge.

By embracing these strategies and trends, brands can grow their online presence, engage with their audience, and achieve long-term success in the digital age.

Chapter 8:

Dan Kennedy Direct Response Marketing

Dan Kennedy, a titan in the world of direct response marketing, has been a significant influence on the field of marketing and advertising for several decades. Known for his practical, no-nonsense approach, Kennedy's strategies have helped countless businesses achieve remarkable success. This section delves into his early life and career, his major contributions to marketing, and his lasting influence on the industry.

Early Life

Dan Kennedy was born on December 3, 1954, in Cleveland, Ohio. From a young age, he exhibited an entrepreneurial spirit and a keen interest in business. His early experiences in various business ventures laid the groundwork for his future career in marketing. Kennedy often cites his challenging upbringing and early struggles as critical factors that shaped his work ethic and determination.

Educational Background

Kennedy's educational journey was unconventional. He did not attend college, opting instead to dive directly into the world of business and marketing. He was largely self-taught, immersing himself in books, seminars, and hands-on experience. His autodidactic approach allowed him to develop a unique perspective on marketing, unbound by traditional academic constraints.

Early Career Ventures

In his early twenties, Kennedy started his first business—a small advertising agency. Despite facing numerous challenges, he quickly realized the potential of direct response marketing. He was drawn to the measurable nature of this approach, where every campaign's effectiveness could be quantified and optimized.

Kennedy's early ventures included copywriting, where he honed his skills in crafting compelling, persuasive messages. His ability to connect with audiences and drive action through his writing became one of his signature strengths. Over time, he developed a reputation as a formidable copywriter and marketing strategist.

Major Contributions to Marketing

Foundational Principles of Direct Response Marketing

One of Kennedy's most significant contributions to marketing is his development and popularization of the foundational principles of direct response marketing. Unlike traditional advertising, which often focuses on building brand awareness, direct response marketing is designed to elicit immediate action from the audience, such as making a purchase, signing up for a newsletter, or requesting more information.

Kennedy's principles include:

Compelling Offers: Creating irresistible offers that motivate the audience to take immediate action. This often involves a combination of urgency, scarcity, and high perceived value.

- Strong Calls to Action: Clearly communicating what action the audience should take and why they should take it now. Effective calls to action are specific, urgent, and benefit-driven.

- Tracking and Measuring: Implementing systems to track and measure the effectiveness of each marketing campaign. This data-driven approach allows for continuous optimization and improvement.

- Targeted Messaging: Crafting messages that speak directly to the needs, desires, and pain points of the target audience. Personalized and relevant messaging increases the likelihood of engagement and response.

Books and Educational Programs

Kennedy has authored numerous books on marketing, copywriting, and entrepreneurship, which have become essential reading for marketers and business owners. Some of his most notable works include:

- "The Ultimate Sales Letter": A comprehensive guide to writing powerful sales letters that convert. This book provides practical tips and examples, making it a valuable resource for both novice and experienced marketers.

- "No B.S. Direct Marketing": This series of books covers various aspects of direct marketing, offering no-nonsense advice and real-world examples. The series includes titles on marketing to the affluent, time management, and social media.

- "The Ultimate Marketing Plan": A step-by-step guide to creating a marketing plan that drives results. This book emphasizes the importance of understanding the target audience and crafting a compelling message.

In addition to his books, Kennedy has developed a range of educational programs and seminars. These programs provide in-depth training on direct response marketing, copywriting, and business growth strategies. His seminars, known for their practical insights and actionable advice, have attracted thousands of attendees over the years.

Consulting and Coaching

Kennedy has also made a significant impact through his consulting and coaching work. He has advised a wide range of clients, from small business owners to large corporations, helping them implement effective direct response marketing strategies. His consulting approach is hands-on and results-oriented, focusing on immediate improvements and long-term success.

One of his most notable contributions is the concept of "Magnetic Marketing," a system designed to attract and retain customers through targeted, compelling messaging. This system has been widely adopted and has helped countless businesses achieve substantial growth.

Influence on the Copywriting Industry

Kennedy's influence extends beyond marketing strategy to the craft of copywriting. He is widely regarded as one of the industry's top copywriters, and his work has set new standards for persuasive writing. His emphasis on understanding the psychology of the audience, crafting compelling narratives, and using proven templates and formulas has inspired a generation of copywriters.

Impact on Small Businesses and Entrepreneurs

Kennedy's work has been particularly impactful for small businesses and entrepreneurs. His practical, results-driven approach provides a clear roadmap for achieving growth and success, even with limited resources. By focusing on direct response marketing, small businesses can compete more effectively and achieve measurable results.

Dan Kennedy's Marketing Strategies

Kennedy's marketing strategies are known for their effectiveness and practicality. Some of his key

strategies include:

Magnetic Marketing: A system that focuses on attracting customers through targeted messaging and compelling offers. This approach emphasizes the importance of understanding the target audience and crafting messages that resonate with their needs and desires.

- Info-Marketing: The practice of creating and selling information products, such as books, courses, and seminars. Kennedy has successfully used this strategy to monetize his expertise and build a loyal following.

- Niche Marketing: Focusing on specific niches and tailoring marketing efforts to meet the unique needs of those audiences. Niche marketing allows for more targeted and effective campaigns.

- Continuity Programs: Developing subscription-based products and services that provide ongoing value to customers. Continuity programs create a steady revenue stream and build long-term customer relationships.

Influence on the Industry

Educational Legacy

Dan Kennedy's influence on the marketing industry is profound and far-reaching. Through his books, seminars, and consulting work, he has educated and inspired countless marketers, entrepreneurs, and business owners. His teachings have become a cornerstone of modern direct response marketing, and his principles are widely adopted and practiced.

Mentorship and Thought Leadership

Kennedy has mentored many of today's leading marketers and business strategists. His mentorship has helped shape the careers of numerous individuals who have gone on to make significant contributions to the industry. As a thought leader, Kennedy's insights and strategies continue to be highly respected and sought after.

Contributions to Direct Response Marketing

Kennedy's contributions to direct response marketing have fundamentally changed the way businesses approach their marketing efforts. His emphasis on measurable results, compelling offers, and targeted messaging has set new standards for effectiveness and accountability. Direct response marketing, once a niche discipline, has become a mainstream strategy thanks to Kennedy's influence.

Innovations in Copywriting

Kennedy's innovations in copywriting have had a lasting impact on the industry. His techniques for crafting persuasive, action-oriented copy are now considered best practices. His teachings have elevated the craft of copywriting, emphasizing the importance of understanding the audience and delivering value through every piece of communication.

Empowerment of Small Businesses

One of Kennedy's most significant contributions is his empowerment of small businesses and entrepreneurs. By providing practical, actionable strategies, he has enabled countless small business owners to achieve success. His focus on direct response marketing offers a clear path to growth, even for those with limited budgets and resources.

Legacy of Results-Oriented Marketing

Kennedy's legacy is defined by his commitment to results-oriented marketing. He has consistently emphasized the importance of tracking and measuring the effectiveness of marketing efforts. This focus on accountability has helped businesses achieve tangible results and maximize their return on investment.

Impact on Marketing Education

Kennedy's work has also influenced the field of marketing education. His books and courses are used as teaching materials in marketing programs around the world. His practical, real-world approach to marketing has made his teachings accessible and valuable to students and professionals alike.
Conclusion

Dan Kennedy's career and contributions to direct response marketing have left an indelible mark on the industry. His practical, results-driven approach has transformed the way businesses approach marketing, emphasizing the importance of compelling offers, strong calls to action, and measurable results. Through his books, seminars, and consulting work, Kennedy has educated and inspired countless marketers, entrepreneurs, and business owners.

His influence extends beyond marketing strategy to the craft of copywriting, where his techniques for persuasive writing have set new standards. Kennedy's impact on small businesses and entrepreneurs is particularly noteworthy, as his practical strategies have empowered countless individuals to achieve success.

Kennedy's legacy is defined by his commitment to results-oriented marketing and his ability to provide clear, actionable guidance. His teachings continue to shape the industry, and his influence is felt by marketers around the world. As a thought leader, mentor, and innovator, Dan Kennedy has cemented his place as one of the most influential figures in the history of marketing.

The Fundamentals of Direct Response Marketing

Direct response marketing is a powerful and precise approach to engaging customers and driving immediate actions. Unlike traditional advertising, which aims to build brand awareness over time, direct response marketing focuses on generating instant, measurable responses from the target audience. This section explores the key principles and tactics of direct response marketing, techniques for crafting effective calls to action, and strategies for measuring response and ROI.

Key Principles and Tactics

1. Direct Engagement

The cornerstone of direct response marketing is direct engagement with the target audience. This involves reaching out to potential customers through various channels, such as direct mail, email, social media, and online ads. The goal is to establish a direct line of communication that encourages immediate interaction.

2. Clear and Compelling Offers

A clear and compelling offer is crucial for motivating the audience to take action. The offer should be relevant, valuable, and easy to understand. It should address a specific need or desire of the target audience and provide a clear benefit. Offers can include discounts, free trials, limited-time promotions, and exclusive access to products or services.

3. Strong Calls to Action (CTAs)

A strong call to action is essential for guiding the audience toward the desired response. CTAs should be specific, urgent, and benefit-driven. They should clearly communicate what action the audience should take and what they will gain by taking it. Examples of effective CTAs include "Buy Now," "Sign Up Today," "Get Your Free Trial," and "Download the Guide."

4. Targeted Messaging

Direct response marketing requires targeted

messaging that resonates with the specific needs and preferences of the audience. This involves segmenting the audience based on demographics, behaviors, and interests and crafting personalized messages that speak directly to each segment.

5. Measurable Results

One of the key advantages of direct response marketing is the ability to measure results accurately. Every campaign should have clear objectives and metrics for success, such as response rates, conversion rates, and return on investment (ROI). This data-driven approach allows marketers to track performance, identify areas for improvement, and optimize future campaigns.

6. Multi-Channel Approach

Utilizing multiple channels can enhance the reach and effectiveness of direct response marketing. Combining channels such as direct mail, email, social media, and online advertising allows marketers to engage the audience at different touchpoints and increase the likelihood of a response. Each channel should be integrated into a cohesive strategy that reinforces the overall message.

7. Continuous Testing and Optimization

Continuous testing and optimization are critical for maximizing the effectiveness of direct response marketing campaigns. This involves experimenting with different elements, such as headlines, offers, CTAs, and layouts, to determine what works best. A/B testing and multivariate testing are common methods used to identify the most effective combinations. Crafting Effective Calls to Action

The call to action (CTA) is a pivotal element in any direct response marketing campaign. It is the prompt that encourages the audience to take the desired action. Crafting an effective CTA requires careful consideration of the language, design, and placement.

1. Clarity and Specificity

A CTA should be clear and specific about what action the audience should take. Vague or ambiguous CTAs can lead to confusion and inaction. For example, instead of saying "Click Here," a more specific CTA would be "Download Your Free eBook Now."

2. Urgency and Scarcity

Creating a sense of urgency and scarcity can motivate the audience to act quickly. Phrases like "Limited Time Offer," "Only a Few Left," and "Offer Ends Soon" convey that the opportunity is time-sensitive and may not be available later.

3. Benefit-Driven Language

The CTA should clearly communicate the benefit of taking action. It should answer the audience's question, "What's in it for me?" For example, a CTA that says "Get 20% Off Your First Purchase" highlights the immediate benefit of a discount.

4. Action-Oriented Verbs

Using action-oriented verbs makes the CTA more dynamic and compelling. Words like "Get," "Download," "Subscribe," "Join," and "Start" encourage the audience to take immediate action.

5. Prominent Placement

The placement of the CTA is crucial for visibility and effectiveness. It should be prominently displayed where the audience can easily see it, such as above the fold on a webpage, at the end of an email, or in the center of a direct mail piece. Multiple CTAs can be used throughout the content to reinforce the desired action.

6. Contrasting Design

The design of the CTA should stand out from the rest of the content. Using contrasting colors, bold fonts, and eye-catching buttons can draw attention to the CTA and make it more noticeable.

7. Personalization

Personalizing the CTA can increase its relevance and effectiveness. Addressing the audience by name or tailoring the CTA to their specific interests can create a more personalized and engaging experience. For example, "John, Start Your Free Trial Today" is more personalized than a generic "Start Your Free Trial Today."

Measuring Response and ROI

Measuring the response and ROI of direct response marketing campaigns is essential for evaluating their effectiveness and making data-driven decisions. Key metrics to track include:

1. Response Rate

The response rate measures the percentage of the audience that takes the desired action in response to the campaign. It is calculated by dividing the number of responses by the total number of recipients and multiplying by 100. For example, if 100 out of 1,000 recipients respond to a direct mail campaign, the response rate is 10%.

2. Conversion Rate

The conversion rate measures the percentage of responders who complete a specific goal, such as making a purchase or signing up for a service. It is calculated by dividing the number of conversions by the total number of responses and multiplying by 100. For example, if 50 out of 100 responders make a purchase, the conversion rate is 50%.

3. Cost Per Response (CPR)

The cost per response measures the cost of generating each response. It is calculated by dividing the total campaign cost by the number of responses. For example, if a campaign costs $1,000 and generates 100 responses, the CPR is $10.

4. Cost Per Conversion (CPC)

The cost per conversion measures the cost of generating each conversion. It is calculated by dividing the total campaign cost by the number of conversions. For example, if a campaign costs $1,000 and generates 50 conversions, the CPC is $20.

5. Return on Investment (ROI)

The ROI measures the profitability of the campaign. It is calculated by subtracting the total campaign cost from the total revenue generated and dividing by the total campaign cost. The result is multiplied by 100 to express it as a percentage. For example, if a campaign generates $5,000 in revenue and costs $1,000, the ROI is 400%.

6. Lifetime Value (LTV)

The LTV measures the total revenue a customer is expected to generate over their lifetime as a customer. This metric helps determine the long-term value of acquiring new customers through direct response marketing. For example, if the average customer generates $1,000 in revenue over their lifetime, the LTV is $1,000.

7. Response Quality

In addition to quantitative metrics, it is important to assess the quality of the responses. This includes evaluating the engagement and satisfaction of responders, as well as the relevance of the leads generated. High-quality responses are more likely to

convert and contribute to long-term success.
Techniques for Crafting Compelling Offers

Crafting compelling offers is a critical component of direct response marketing. An irresistible offer captures the audience's attention, addresses their needs and desires, and motivates them to take action. This section explores techniques for creating irresistible offers, testing and optimizing offers, and provides examples of successful campaigns.

Creating Irresistible Offers

1. Understand the Audience

The foundation of a compelling offer is a deep understanding of the target audience. This involves researching their needs, desires, pain points, and preferences. By understanding what motivates the audience, marketers can craft offers that resonate and provide genuine value.

2. Highlight Benefits

The offer should clearly highlight the benefits the audience will receive. This includes both tangible benefits, such as discounts and free trials, and intangible benefits, such as convenience, peace of mind, and exclusivity. The benefits should be prominently featured in the offer to make it immediately appealing.

3. Create a Sense of Urgency

Urgency encourages the audience to act quickly rather

than delaying their decision. Techniques for creating urgency include limited-time offers, countdown timers, and scarcity messages (e.g., "Only 5 left in stock"). Urgency creates a fear of missing out (FOMO) that can drive immediate action.

4. Offer Incentives

Incentives can make the offer more attractive and motivate the audience to take action. Common incentives include discounts, free gifts, bonuses, and exclusive access. The incentive should be relevant to the audience and provide additional value.

5. Simplify the Process

The process for redeeming the offer should be simple and straightforward. Complicated or time-consuming processes can deter the audience from taking action. Clear instructions, minimal steps, and user-friendly interfaces help ensure a smooth experience.

6. Use Social Proof

Social proof, such as testimonials, reviews, and case studies, can enhance the credibility and appeal of the offer. Positive feedback from satisfied customers reassures the audience that the offer is valuable and trustworthy. Highlighting social proof can increase confidence and drive responses.

7. Personalize the Offer

Personalizing the offer can make it more relevant and engaging for the audience. Personalization can include addressing the audience by name, tailoring the offer to their specific interests, and providing customized recommendations. Personalization creates a more meaningful connection with the audience.

Testing and Optimizing Offers

Continuous testing and optimization are essential for maximizing the effectiveness of offers. This involves experimenting with different elements, analyzing results, and making data-driven adjustments.

Common techniques for testing and optimizing offers include:

1. A/B Testing

A/B testing involves comparing two versions of an offer to determine which one performs better. This can include testing different headlines, CTAs, images, and incentives. By measuring the performance of each version, marketers can identify the most effective elements and refine their offers.

2. Multivariate Testing

Multivariate testing is a more advanced technique that involves testing multiple variables simultaneously. This allows marketers to understand how different elements interact and identify the optimal combination. Multivariate testing provides deeper insights but requires a larger sample size.

3. Segmenting the Audience

Segmenting the audience allows marketers to test offers on specific groups and tailor the offers to their unique needs and preferences. This can include segmenting by demographics, behaviors, and interests. Segmenting enables more targeted testing and optimization.

4. Analyzing Metrics

Analyzing key metrics, such as response rates, conversion rates, and ROI, provides insights into the effectiveness of offers. By tracking these metrics, marketers can identify trends, measure the impact of changes, and make data-driven decisions. Regular analysis helps ensure that offers remain relevant and effective.

5. Iterative Refinement

Iterative refinement involves making incremental adjustments to the offer based on testing results and feedback. This continuous improvement process allows marketers to optimize offers over time and achieve better results. Iterative refinement ensures that offers evolve to meet changing audience needs and market conditions.

6. Gathering Feedback

Gathering feedback from responders provides valuable insights into the strengths and weaknesses of the offer. This can include surveys, interviews, and user reviews. Feedback helps identify areas for improvement and informs future offer development. Examples of Successful Campaigns

1. Dollar Shave Club

Dollar Shave Club is a prime example of a successful direct response marketing campaign. The company's launch video, titled "Our Blades Are F***ing Great," went viral and generated millions of views. The video featured a compelling offer of high-quality razors delivered to the customer's door for just $1 per month.

Key Elements:

- Clear and Compelling Offer: The offer was straightforward and provided clear value—affordable razors delivered conveniently.

- Strong CTA: The video included a clear call to action to sign up for the service.

- Humor and Relatability: The video used humor and relatable messaging to engage the audience and create a memorable impression.

Results:

The campaign resulted in a massive influx of subscribers, and Dollar Shave Club quickly became a major player in the razor market. The company's success demonstrated the power of a compelling offer combined with effective direct response marketing.

2. Airbnb

Airbnb's "Night At" campaign offered unique, one-of-a-kind experiences, such as spending a night at the Great Wall of China or an underwater bedroom in the Great Barrier Reef. These offers were designed to capture the imagination of the audience and drive engagement.

Key Elements:

- Unique and Irresistible Offer: The experiences were exclusive and highly desirable, creating a strong appeal.

- Urgency and Scarcity: The limited availability of the experiences created a sense of urgency and FOMO.

- Strong CTA: The campaigns included clear calls to action to enter the contest or book the experience.

Results:

The "Night At" campaigns generated significant media coverage, social media buzz, and engagement. They helped position Airbnb as a provider of unique and memorable experiences, enhancing the brand's appeal and driving bookings.

3. Blue Apron

Blue Apron, a meal kit delivery service, used direct response marketing to grow its customer base. The company's offers included discounts on the first few orders and free trial meals to entice new customers to try the service.

Key Elements:

- Compelling Incentives: Discounts and free trials provided a low-risk way for customers to experience the service.

- Personalization: The offers were personalized based on customer preferences and dietary needs.

- Multi-Channel Approach: Blue Apron used email, social media, and online ads to reach potential customers.

Results:

The campaigns successfully attracted a large number of new customers, many of whom became long-term subscribers. Blue Apron's direct response marketing strategies helped establish the company as a leader in the meal kit delivery industry.

Direct response marketing is a powerful approach that focuses on generating immediate, measurable actions from the audience. By adhering to key principles and tactics, crafting effective calls to action, and continuously testing and optimizing offers, marketers can create compelling campaigns that drive results.

Crafting irresistible offers requires a deep understanding of the audience, highlighting benefits, creating urgency, offering incentives, simplifying the process, using social proof, and personalizing the offer. Testing and optimizing offers through A/B testing, multivariate testing, segmenting the audience, analyzing metrics, iterative refinement, and gathering feedback ensures that offers remain relevant and effective.

Successful campaigns, such as those by Dollar Shave Club, Airbnb, and Blue Apron, demonstrate the impact of well-crafted offers and direct response marketing strategies. By leveraging these techniques, businesses can achieve significant growth and build strong, lasting relationships with their customers.

The Fundamentals of Direct Response Marketing

Direct response marketing is a powerful strategy that focuses on eliciting an immediate response from the target audience. Unlike traditional advertising, which aims to build brand awareness over time, direct response marketing seeks to drive specific actions, such as making a purchase, signing up for a newsletter, or requesting more information. This approach is highly measurable and can provide clear insights into the return on investment (ROI).

Key Principles and Tactics

1. Clear and Compelling Messaging

- The foundation of any successful direct response campaign is a clear, compelling message that resonates with the target audience. This message should address the needs, desires, and pain points of the audience and offer a solution that is both desirable and achievable.

2. Strong Calls to Action (CTAs)

- An effective direct response campaign includes a strong call to action (CTA). The CTA should be clear, concise, and compelling, encouraging the audience to take the desired action immediately. Phrases like "Buy Now," "Subscribe Today," or "Get Your Free Trial" are examples of effective CTAs.

3. Personalization

- Personalization involves tailoring the message and offer to the individual recipient. This can include using the recipient's name, referencing past purchases, or suggesting products based on previous behavior. Personalization can significantly increase response rates by making the offer more relevant and engaging.

4. Urgency and Scarcity

- Creating a sense of urgency or scarcity can drive immediate action. Limited-time offers, countdown timers, and statements like "Only a few left in stock" can encourage the audience to act quickly to avoid missing out.

5. Multi-Channel Integration

- Utilizing multiple channels, such as email, social media, direct mail, and online advertising, can increase the reach and effectiveness of a direct response campaign. Each channel should be optimized for the specific audience and platform to maximize engagement.

6. Testing and Optimization

- Continuous testing and optimization are crucial for improving the performance of direct response campaigns. This includes A/B testing different messages, offers, and CTAs, as well as analyzing the results to identify what works best.

7. Tracking and Analytics

- Accurate tracking and analytics are essential for measuring the success of direct response campaigns. This involves setting up tracking mechanisms to monitor responses and conversions and using analytics tools to assess the effectiveness of different tactics and channels.

Crafting Effective Calls to Action

A call to action (CTA) is a critical component of any direct response marketing campaign. It prompts the audience to take a specific action, such as making a purchase or signing up for a service. Crafting an effective CTA involves several key elements:

1. Clarity

The CTA should be clear and easy to understand. Avoid jargon or complex language that might confuse the audience. Simple, direct phrases like "Shop Now" or "Download Free Guide" are more effective.

2. Visibility

The CTA should be prominently displayed and easy to find. This can be achieved through strategic placement, contrasting colors, and bold fonts. Ensure that the CTA stands out from the rest of the content.

3. Relevance

The CTA should be relevant to the content and the audience. It should align with the overall message and offer a clear benefit to the audience. For example, a CTA for a free trial should emphasize the value of trying the product without commitment.

4. Urgency

Creating a sense of urgency can motivate the audience to act quickly. Phrases like "Limited Time Offer," "Act Now," or "Offer Expires Soon" can encourage immediate action.

5. Incentives

Offering an incentive can increase the likelihood of response. This can include discounts, free shipping, or a free gift with purchase. The incentive should be clearly stated in the CTA to entice the audience.

Measuring Response and ROI

Measuring the response and ROI of direct response marketing campaigns is essential for evaluating their effectiveness and optimizing future efforts. This involves several key steps:

1. Setting Clear Objectives

Define clear objectives for the campaign, such as the number of sales, sign-ups, or leads generated. These objectives will serve as benchmarks for measuring success.

2. Tracking Responses

Use tracking mechanisms, such as unique URLs, promo codes, or tracking pixels, to monitor responses. This will allow you to attribute responses to specific campaigns and channels.

3. Analyzing Data

Analyze the data to assess the performance of different tactics and channels. Look at metrics such as conversion rates, cost per acquisition (CPA), and return on ad spend (ROAS) to determine the effectiveness of the campaign.

4. Calculating ROI

Calculate the ROI by comparing the revenue

generated by the campaign to the costs incurred. This will provide a clear picture of the campaign's profitability and help identify areas for improvement.

5. Making Data-Driven Decisions

Use the insights gained from the analysis to make data-driven decisions for future campaigns. This may involve adjusting the messaging, offer, or targeting to improve performance.

Techniques for Crafting Compelling Offers

Creating compelling offers is a critical aspect of direct response marketing. A compelling offer can significantly increase the likelihood of response and conversion. Here are some techniques for crafting irresistible offers:

Creating Irresistible Offers

1. Understand the Audience

To create an irresistible offer, it is essential to understand the needs, desires, and pain points of the target audience. Conduct market research and gather insights to identify what motivates the audience and what they value most.

2. Highlight Unique Selling Propositions (USPs)

Emphasize the unique features and benefits of the product or service that set it apart from competitors. Highlighting USPs can make the offer more attractive and persuade the audience to choose your product over others.

3. Offer Value

Ensure that the offer provides clear value to the audience. This can include discounts, free trials, bonuses, or exclusive access to premium content. The perceived value of the offer should outweigh the cost to the audience.

4. Use Social Proof

Incorporate social proof, such as customer testimonials, reviews, and case studies, to build credibility and trust. Social proof can reassure the audience that others have benefited from the offer and that it is worth pursuing.

5. Create a Sense of Urgency

Encourage immediate action by creating a sense of urgency. This can be achieved through limited-time offers, countdown timers, and statements like "Hurry, while supplies last."

6. Simplify the Process

Make it easy for the audience to take advantage of the offer. Simplify the process by minimizing the steps required and providing clear instructions. A complicated process can deter potential customers from responding.

Testing and Optimizing Offers

Testing and optimizing offers is an ongoing process that involves continuously refining and improving the offer to maximize response and conversion rates. Here are some key techniques for testing and optimizing offers:

1. A/B Testing

Conduct A/B testing to compare different versions of the offer and identify which one performs better. This can involve testing different headlines, CTAs, visuals, and incentives. Use the insights gained from the tests to optimize the offer.

2. Multivariate Testing

Multivariate testing involves testing multiple elements of the offer simultaneously to determine the best combination. This can provide more comprehensive insights and help optimize the entire offer.

3. Segment Testing

Test different offers with different audience segments to identify what resonates best with each group. This can involve testing offers based on demographics, behavior, or preferences. Tailoring offers to specific segments can increase relevance and response rates.

4. Monitor Performance Metrics

Continuously monitor performance metrics, such as conversion rates, CPA, and ROAS, to assess the effectiveness of the offer. Use the data to identify areas for improvement and make data-driven adjustments.

5. Iterate and Improve

Use the insights gained from testing and monitoring to iterate and improve the offer. Continuously refine the offer based on what works best and keep experimenting with new ideas and approaches.

Examples of Successful Campaigns

1. Dropbox's Referral Program

Dropbox's referral program is a classic example of a successful direct response campaign. By offering free storage space to both the referrer and the referee, Dropbox incentivized users to invite others to join the platform. This simple yet effective offer drove exponential growth and helped Dropbox achieve millions of users.

2. Dollar Shave Club's Viral Video

Dollar Shave Club's launch campaign featured a humorous and engaging video that went viral. The video highlighted the company's unique value proposition—high-quality razors delivered to your door for just a few dollars a month. The compelling offer and entertaining content led to a surge in sign-ups and rapid growth for the company.

3. Airbnb's Personalized Email Campaigns

Airbnb uses personalized email campaigns to target users based on their search history and preferences. By offering personalized recommendations and exclusive deals, Airbnb creates a compelling offer that encourages users to book their next stay. The personalized approach has helped increase engagement and bookings.

4. Groupon's Daily Deals

Groupon's daily deals offer significant discounts on local experiences, products, and services. The limited-time nature of the offers creates a sense of urgency, encouraging users to act quickly. This approach has made Groupon a leader in the deals and discounts space, driving high response rates and customer engagement.

5. Amazon's Prime Membership

Amazon's Prime membership offers a range of benefits, including free two-day shipping, access to streaming services, and exclusive deals. The comprehensive value proposition and the convenience of the benefits make Prime an irresistible offer for many customers. This has led to high subscription rates and strong customer loyalty.

Direct response marketing is a powerful and measurable approach to driving immediate action and achieving specific marketing objectives. By understanding and applying the key principles and tactics, crafting effective calls to action, and measuring response and ROI, businesses can create successful direct response campaigns. Additionally, by employing techniques for crafting compelling offers, testing and optimizing offers, and learning from successful campaigns, businesses can continuously improve their direct response marketing efforts and achieve better results.

Chapter 9:

Rosser Reeves The Unique Selling Proposition

Rosser Reeves was a towering figure in the advertising world, renowned for his development of the Unique Selling Proposition (USP). His approach revolutionized advertising by focusing on the distinct benefits of a product, a strategy that has become a cornerstone of modern marketing.

Early Life and Career

Rosser Reeves was born on September 10, 1910, in Danville, Virginia. From a young age, Reeves exhibited a keen interest in language and persuasion, skills that would later define his career in advertising. He attended the University of Virginia, where he studied literature and philosophy, disciplines that honed his analytical thinking and creativity.

After graduating, Reeves embarked on his advertising career during the Great Depression, a time when the industry was undergoing significant changes. His first job was at the New York-based ad agency Ted Bates & Company, where he started as a copywriter. It was here that Reeves began to develop his distinctive style, focusing on clear, direct, and impactful messaging.

Major Campaigns and Achievements

Reeves' career was marked by numerous successful campaigns that not only boosted sales for his clients but also left a lasting impact on the advertising industry. His work at Ted Bates & Company exemplified his ability to craft messages that resonated with consumers and drove results.

One of Reeves' most notable campaigns was for Anacin, a pain reliever. Prior to Reeves' involvement, Anacin was one of many similar products in a crowded market. Reeves identified a unique selling point: Anacin's combination of aspirin, caffeine, and a buffering agent. He developed the slogan "Fast, fast, fast relief," emphasizing the speed and efficacy of the product. This campaign transformed Anacin into a market leader, demonstrating the power of a well-crafted USP.

Another significant campaign was for M&M's, the popular candy. Reeves coined the famous slogan "Melts in your mouth, not in your hand." This catchy phrase highlighted a specific benefit of the product, setting M&M's apart from competitors and embedding the brand deeply into popular culture.

Reeves also worked on campaigns for Colgate toothpaste, crafting the slogan "Cleans your breath while it cleans your teeth." This dual benefit approach showcased his knack for identifying and communicating multiple unique selling points in a simple and memorable way.

Influence on the Advertising Industry

Reeves' most enduring contribution to advertising is the concept of the Unique Selling Proposition (USP). The USP is a clear, concise statement that articulates the unique benefit of a product or service, answering the consumer's question: "Why should I buy this product instead of any other?" Reeves' insistence on the USP transformed advertising from a creative art into a strategic science.

The Principles of USP

- Uniqueness: The USP must highlight a feature or benefit that is unique to the product, something that competitors do not offer. This uniqueness can be a product feature, a manufacturing process, or even a brand promise.

- Selling: The USP must be compelling and persuasive, capable of convincing the consumer that the product offers superior value. It should address a specific need or solve a particular problem that the consumer faces.

- Proposition: The USP should be a proposition that is clearly communicated and easily understood. It must be direct and unambiguous, leaving no room for confusion about what the product offers.

Reeves' approach was often criticized for being formulaic and repetitive, but its effectiveness was undeniable. His campaigns consistently delivered results, driving sales and building brand loyalty. Reeves argued that advertising's primary function was to sell and that creativity should serve this goal rather than exist for its own sake.

Impact on Modern Advertising

Reeves' influence on modern advertising is profound. His focus on clear, benefit-driven messaging has become a fundamental principle in the industry. Marketers today continue to use the USP framework to develop campaigns that differentiate their products in competitive markets.

The digital age has only amplified the relevance of Reeves' principles. In a world where consumers are bombarded with advertising across multiple platforms, a clear and compelling USP can cut through the noise and capture attention. The success of direct response marketing, content marketing, and digital advertising often hinges on the ability to articulate a strong USP.

Legacy and Recognition

Rosser Reeves' legacy extends beyond his campaigns and the USP. He authored the book "Reality in Advertising," published in 1961, which became a seminal text in the field. In it, Reeves elaborated on his advertising philosophy and provided insights into his methods and successes. The book remains a valuable resource for marketers and advertisers, illustrating the timeless principles of effective advertising.

Reeves' contributions have been recognized with numerous awards and accolades. He was inducted into the Advertising Hall of Fame, and his work continues to be studied and admired by industry professionals and academics alike.

Rosser Reeves' pioneering work in advertising, particularly his development of the Unique Selling Proposition, has left an indelible mark on the industry. His ability to distill a product's unique benefits into a compelling and persuasive message revolutionized advertising and set new standards for effectiveness and clarity. Reeves' legacy lives on in the principles and practices that continue to drive successful advertising campaigns today.

Understanding the Unique Selling Proposition (USP)

The concept of the Unique Selling Proposition (USP) is fundamental in the world of marketing and advertising. It serves as a cornerstone for distinguishing a product or service from its competitors, providing a clear reason why consumers should choose it over others.

Definition and Importance of USP

Definition of USP

A Unique Selling Proposition (USP) is a distinct benefit or feature of a product or service that sets it apart from competitors. It is a compelling, concise statement that communicates the unique value the product offers to the consumer. The USP answers the critical question: "Why should I buy this product instead of any other?"

Importance of USP

The importance of a USP cannot be overstated. In today's saturated markets, where consumers are bombarded with countless options, a strong USP can be the deciding factor in a purchase decision. Here are several reasons why a USP is crucial:

- Differentiation: A USP clearly differentiates a product from its competitors. By highlighting unique features or benefits, it helps the product stand out in the marketplace.

- Clarity: A USP provides a clear and concise message about what the product offers. This clarity helps consumers quickly understand the value of the product and how it meets their needs.

- Focus: Developing a USP forces businesses to focus on their strengths and what makes them unique. This focus can guide marketing strategies, product development, and overall business operations.

- Trust and Credibility: A strong USP can build trust and credibility with consumers. By consistently delivering on the promises made in the USP, businesses can establish a loyal customer base.

- Competitive Advantage: A compelling USP provides a competitive advantage by offering something that competitors do not. This can lead to increased market share and higher profitability.

Crafting a Strong USP

Crafting a strong USP involves several key steps. It requires a deep understanding of the target market, the product, and the competitive landscape. Here are the essential steps to create an effective USP:

1. Know Your Audience

Understanding the target audience is the first step in crafting a strong USP. This involves identifying their needs, desires, pain points, and preferences. Market research, surveys, and customer feedback can provide valuable insights into what the audience values most.

2. Analyze Competitors

Conduct a thorough analysis of competitors to identify what they offer and how they position themselves in the market. Look for gaps or areas where your product can offer something unique. Understanding competitors' USPs can also help avoid overlapping and ensure your USP is truly distinctive.

3. Identify Unique Benefits

Identify the unique benefits and features of your product that set it apart from competitors. This could be a specific function, superior quality, exceptional service, innovative technology, or any other aspect that adds significant value to the consumer.

4. Focus on Benefits, Not Features

While features describe what a product does, benefits explain how those features improve the consumer's life. A strong USP focuses on the benefits, clearly articulating how the product solves a problem or fulfills a need. For example, instead of highlighting a car's advanced braking system (feature), the USP should emphasize the enhanced safety it provides (benefit).

5. Keep It Simple and Clear

A USP should be simple, clear, and easy to understand. Avoid jargon and complex language that might confuse the audience. The message should be concise and direct, making it easy for consumers to grasp the unique value proposition quickly.

6. Make It Memorable

A memorable USP sticks in the minds of consumers and becomes associated with the brand. Use catchy phrases, slogans, or taglines that are easy to recall. Memorable USPs can become powerful marketing tools that drive brand recognition and loyalty.

7. Validate the USP

Before finalizing the USP, test it with a sample of the target audience to ensure it resonates with them. Gather feedback and make necessary adjustments to refine the message. A validated USP is more likely to be effective in the broader market.

Communicating the USP Effectively

Once a strong USP is crafted, effectively communicating it to the target audience is crucial. Here are some strategies for effectively communicating the USP:

1. Consistent Messaging

Ensure that the USP is consistently communicated across all marketing channels and touchpoints. Consistency reinforces the message and helps build brand recognition. Whether it's on the website, in advertising campaigns, social media, or packaging, the USP should be prominently featured and consistently articulated.

2. Visual Elements

Visual elements, such as logos, colors, and imagery, can enhance the communication of the USP. Use visuals that complement and reinforce the message. For example, a USP focused on natural ingredients can be supported by using earthy colors and images of nature.

3. Storytelling

Storytelling is a powerful way to communicate the USP. Share stories that illustrate the unique benefits of the product and how it has positively impacted customers' lives. Stories can make the USP more relatable and engaging, creating an emotional connection with the audience.

4. Customer Testimonials and Reviews

Customer testimonials and reviews provide social proof and credibility to the USP. Highlight positive feedback from satisfied customers that align with the USP. This can build trust and reassure potential customers that the product delivers on its promises.

5. Multi-Channel Approach

Utilize a multi-channel approach to reach a broader audience. Communicate the USP through various channels, such as online advertising, email marketing, social media, content marketing, and traditional media. Each channel should be optimized to effectively convey the USP to its specific audience.

6. Employee Training

Ensure that employees understand the USP and can communicate it effectively. This is particularly important for customer-facing roles, such as sales and customer service. When employees are well-versed in the USP, they can reinforce the message and provide a consistent experience to customers.

7. Continuous Reinforcement

Reinforce the USP continuously to keep it top of mind for consumers. Use frequent reminders in marketing materials, advertising campaigns, and customer communications. Continuous reinforcement helps build familiarity and strengthens the association between the USP and the brand.

Creating and Communicating a Strong USP

Creating and communicating a strong USP involves identifying unique benefits, employing differentiation strategies, and learning from effective case studies. Identifying Unique Benefits

Identifying unique benefits is the foundation of a strong USP. Here are some strategies to uncover the unique benefits of a product:

1. Conduct Market Research

Conduct market research to understand consumer needs, preferences, and pain points. Use surveys, focus groups, and interviews to gather insights directly from the target audience. Analyze the data to identify common themes and areas where your product can offer unique value.

2. Analyze Product Features

List all the features of the product and analyze how each feature benefits the consumer. Consider both functional benefits (what the product does) and emotional benefits (how the product makes the consumer feel). Look for features that are unique or superior to those offered by competitors.

3. Identify Core Strengths

Identify the core strengths of the product and the brand. This could include proprietary technology, exceptional craftsmanship, superior customer service, or a strong brand reputation. Highlighting these strengths can help differentiate the product in the market.

4. Gather Customer Feedback

Gather feedback from existing customers to understand what they value most about the product. Look for positive comments and testimonials that highlight unique benefits. Use this feedback to inform and validate the USP.

5. Analyze Competitors

Analyze competitors' products and USPs to identify gaps or areas where your product offers something different or better. Understanding the competitive landscape can help pinpoint unique benefits that can be leveraged in the USP.

6. Focus on the Consumer

Always keep the consumer at the center of the process. Think about what matters most to them and how your product can meet their needs in a unique way. A consumer-centric approach ensures that the USP resonates with the target audience.

Differentiation Strategies

Differentiation is essential for creating a strong USP. Here are some strategies to differentiate a product in the market:

1. Product Innovation

Innovate and introduce new features or improvements that set the product apart from competitors. This could include advanced technology, better materials, or unique designs. Product innovation can create a strong competitive advantage.

2. Quality and Performance

Emphasize superior quality and performance. If the product is more durable, reliable, or efficient than competitors, highlight these attributes in the USP. Consumers are often willing to pay a premium for higher quality.

3. Customer Experience

Focus on providing an exceptional customer experience. This includes excellent customer service, easy and enjoyable purchase processes, and strong post-purchase support. A superior customer experience can differentiate the brand and build loyalty.

4. Brand Values

Communicate the brand's values and mission. If the brand is committed to sustainability, ethical practices, or social responsibility, highlight these values in the USP. Consumers increasingly prefer brands that align with their values.

5. Price and Value

Differentiate based on price and value. This could involve offering a premium product at a competitive price or providing excellent value for money. Ensure that the perceived value of the product justifies the price.

6. Niche Focus

Target a specific niche or segment of the market. Tailoring the product and messaging to a niche audience can create a strong USP that resonates deeply with that group. A niche focus can also reduce direct competition.

Case Studies of Effective USPs

Examining successful case studies can provide valuable insights into creating and communicating a strong USP. Here are some examples of effective USPs:

1. Domino's Pizza

USP: "You get fresh, hot pizza delivered to your door in 30 minutes or less—or it's free."

Domino's Pizza revolutionized the fast-food industry with its USP, focusing on fast delivery and customer satisfaction. The promise of hot, fresh pizza delivered quickly addressed a specific need and set Domino's apart from other pizza chains. The USP was simple, clear, and compelling, leading to significant growth and brand loyalty.

2. FedEx

USP: "When it absolutely, positively has to be there overnight."

FedEx's USP emphasized reliability and speed, two critical factors for shipping and logistics. By guaranteeing overnight delivery, FedEx positioned itself as the go-to choice for urgent shipments. The USP built trust and credibility, making FedEx a leader in the industry.

3. M&M's

USP: "Melts in your mouth, not in your hand."

M&M's unique candy coating was highlighted in its USP, differentiating it from other chocolates that could melt easily. The catchy and memorable slogan emphasized a specific benefit, making M&M's a popular choice for consumers looking for a convenient and mess-free treat.

4. Apple

USP: "Think Different."

Apple's USP focused on innovation, creativity, and challenging the status quo. The slogan "Think Different" resonated with consumers who saw themselves as forward-thinking and unique. This USP helped Apple build a strong brand identity and attract a loyal customer base.

5. Volvo

USP: "For life."

Volvo's USP centered on safety, durability, and reliability. The slogan "For life" conveyed the message that Volvo cars are built to protect and last, appealing to consumers who prioritize safety and long-term value. This USP established Volvo as a leader in automotive safety.

6. De Beers

USP: "A diamond is forever."

De Beers' USP created a powerful association between diamonds and eternal love. The slogan "A diamond is forever" positioned diamonds as the ultimate symbol of enduring commitment, driving demand for engagement rings and establishing De Beers as the dominant player in the diamond industry.

7. Nike

USP: "Just Do It."

Nike's USP encouraged consumers to take action and embrace sports and fitness. The slogan "Just Do It" was motivational and empowering, resonating with athletes and fitness enthusiasts. This USP helped Nike become a leading brand in the sportswear market.

The Unique Selling Proposition (USP) is a critical element of successful marketing and advertising. It provides a clear and compelling reason for consumers to choose a product or service over competitors. Crafting a strong USP involves understanding the target audience, identifying unique benefits, and focusing on benefits rather than features. Effectively communicating the USP through consistent messaging, visual elements, storytelling, and multi-channel approaches ensures that the message resonates with the audience and drives results. By learning from successful case studies and employing differentiation strategies, businesses can create and communicate a strong USP that sets them apart in the market and builds lasting brand loyalty.

Case Studies of Campaigns Featuring Effective USPs

Analyzing Successful USP Campaigns

Analyzing successful campaigns featuring effective Unique Selling Propositions (USPs) provides valuable insights into how distinct benefits can drive marketing success. Here, we explore several notable campaigns to understand their strategies and outcomes.

1. Apple's "Think Different" Campaign

Campaign Overview:
Launched in 1997, Apple's "Think Different" campaign marked a significant turning point for the company. At a time when Apple was struggling, this campaign redefined its brand image and appealed to a broad audience of creative professionals and tech enthusiasts.

USP:

"Think Different" positioned Apple as a brand for innovative, forward-thinking individuals who challenge the status quo.

Analysis:

- Emotional Appeal: The campaign leveraged the power of emotional branding by associating Apple with famous innovators and visionaries like Albert Einstein and Mahatma Gandhi.

- Simplicity and Clarity: The slogan was simple yet powerful, effectively communicating a clear message of creativity and innovation.

- Visual and Verbal Consistency: The campaign maintained consistent visual and verbal messaging across all platforms, reinforcing the USP.

Outcome:

The "Think Different" campaign successfully revitalized Apple's brand, leading to increased sales and market share. It laid the foundation for the launch of groundbreaking products like the iMac, iPod, and iPhone.

2. De Beers' "A Diamond is Forever" Campaign

Campaign Overview:

In 1947, De Beers launched the "A Diamond is Forever" campaign, which transformed the diamond industry and cemented diamonds as the ultimate symbol of love and commitment.

USP:

"A Diamond is Forever" positioned diamonds as timeless symbols of eternal love and commitment.

Analysis:

- Cultural Impact: The campaign created a powerful cultural narrative that linked diamonds with the institution of marriage.

- Emotional Resonance: By emphasizing the enduring nature of diamonds, the campaign tapped into deep-seated emotions related to love and commitment.

- Long-Term Consistency: The USP was consistently used over decades, reinforcing the association between diamonds and everlasting love.

Outcome:

The campaign dramatically increased diamond sales worldwide and established De Beers as the leading diamond company. The phrase "A Diamond is Forever" became one of the most recognized advertising slogans in history.

3. Federal Express' "When it Absolutely, Positively Has to be There Overnight" Campaign

Campaign Overview:

Federal Express (now FedEx) launched this campaign in the late 1970s, highlighting its reliable overnight delivery service.

USP:

"When it absolutely, positively has to be there overnight" positioned FedEx as the most reliable option for urgent deliveries.

Analysis:

- Clear and Specific: The USP clearly articulated the core benefit of FedEx's service – guaranteed overnight delivery.

- Trust and Reliability: The campaign built trust by emphasizing reliability and dependability, critical factors for business customers.

- Repetition and Reinforcement: Consistent use of the slogan reinforced FedEx's reputation for reliability.

Outcome:

The campaign established FedEx as a leader in the logistics and delivery industry, significantly boosting its market share and brand loyalty.

4. M&M's "Melts in Your Mouth, Not in Your Hand" Campaign

Campaign Overview:

M&M's introduced this campaign in 1954 to highlight the unique feature of its candy coating.

USP:

"Melts in your mouth, not in your hand" emphasized the convenience and mess-free nature of M&M's.

Analysis:

- Unique Product Feature: The USP focused on a distinctive product feature that directly addressed a common consumer concern.

- Memorable and Catchy: The slogan was easy to remember and became synonymous with the brand.

- Visual Reinforcement: Advertising visuals consistently showcased the USP, reinforcing the message.

Outcome:

The campaign significantly boosted M&M's popularity and sales, making it one of the best-selling candies globally.

Lessons Learned from These Campaigns

Analyzing these successful campaigns reveals several key lessons:

1. Emotional Connection:
Effective USPs often create an emotional connection with the audience. By appealing to emotions, brands can build stronger relationships with consumers and foster loyalty.

2. Clarity and Simplicity:
A strong USP is clear and simple, making it easy for consumers to understand the unique benefit of the product. Avoiding complexity ensures that the message is quickly grasped and remembered.

3. Consistency:
Consistent use of the USP across all marketing channels reinforces the message and builds brand recognition. Long-term consistency helps establish a strong brand identity.

4. Focus on Unique Benefits:
Highlighting unique product features or benefits that competitors do not offer can effectively differentiate a brand in the market.

5. Cultural Relevance:
Successful USPs often tap into cultural narratives or societal values, making the brand more relevant and resonant with consumers.

Modern Examples of Strong USPs

1. Tesla's "Electric Performance with Zero Emissions"
Campaign Overview:

Tesla has positioned itself as a leader in the electric vehicle market with a USP that combines high performance with environmental sustainability.

USP:

"Electric performance with zero emissions" emphasizes the dual benefits of superior driving performance and environmental responsibility.

Analysis:

- Innovation and Sustainability: The USP highlights Tesla's innovative technology and commitment to sustainability, appealing to eco-conscious consumers.

- Performance and Luxury: By combining environmental benefits with high performance, Tesla targets both environmentally conscious and luxury car buyers.

- Brand Identity: The USP is integral to Tesla's brand identity, reinforcing its position as a pioneer in the electric vehicle industry.

Outcome:

Tesla's strong USP has driven significant growth, brand loyalty, and market leadership in the electric vehicle sector.

2. Amazon Prime's "Free Two-Day Shipping and More"

Campaign Overview:

Amazon Prime's USP focuses on the convenience and value provided by its membership program.

USP:

"Free two-day shipping and more" highlights the key benefits of fast shipping and additional services like streaming and exclusive deals.

Analysis:

- Convenience and Value: The USP emphasizes convenience and value, key factors that attract and retain customers.

- Membership Benefits: By bundling multiple benefits, Amazon creates a compelling value proposition for its Prime members.

- Retention and Loyalty: The USP encourages customer retention and loyalty by offering ongoing value through the membership.

Outcome:

Amazon Prime's strong USP has driven massive membership growth, increased customer retention, and contributed significantly to Amazon's overall success.

3. Warby Parker's "Buy a Pair, Give a Pair"

Campaign Overview:

Warby Parker's USP combines affordability with social responsibility, appealing to socially conscious consumers.

USP:

"Buy a pair, give a pair" emphasizes the company's commitment to donating a pair of glasses for every pair purchased.

Analysis:

- Social Impact: The USP highlights Warby Parker's social impact, appealing to consumers who value corporate social responsibility.

- Affordability and Quality: By offering affordable, high-quality eyewear, the company addresses a key consumer need while differentiating itself from traditional eyewear retailers.

- Brand Purpose: The USP reinforces Warby

Parker's brand purpose, building a strong emotional connection with customers.

Outcome:

The campaign has driven significant brand loyalty and growth, establishing Warby Parker as a leader in the eyewear industry with a strong social mission.

Applying USP Concepts to Modern Marketing Challenges

Adapting USPs for digital marketing, integrating USPs into brand strategy, and overcoming common challenges are essential for leveraging the power of USPs in today's dynamic marketing landscape.

Adapting USPs for Digital Marketing

1. Personalization:
Digital marketing allows for highly personalized messaging. Tailor the USP to individual consumer segments based on their preferences, behaviors, and demographics. Personalized USPs can enhance relevance and engagement.

2. Multi-Channel Consistency:
Ensure the USP is consistently communicated across all digital channels, including social media, email marketing, search engine marketing, and content marketing. Consistent messaging reinforces the brand and improves recall.

3. Visual and Interactive Content:
Leverage visual and interactive content to

communicate the USP effectively. Videos, infographics, interactive quizzes, and user-generated content can make the USP more engaging and memorable.

4. Data-Driven Insights:
Utilize data analytics to measure the effectiveness of the USP and make data-driven adjustments. Track key metrics such as click-through rates, conversion rates, and engagement levels to optimize the USP for better performance.

5. Social Proof:
Incorporate social proof, such as customer reviews, testimonials, and influencer endorsements, to strengthen the credibility of the USP. Social proof can enhance trust and persuade potential customers to choose your product.

Integrating USPs into Brand Strategy

1. Brand Positioning:
Integrate the USP into the overall brand positioning to ensure it aligns with the brand's values, mission, and vision. The USP should reflect the core essence of the brand and resonate with its target audience.

2. Consistent Brand Messaging:
Maintain consistent brand messaging across all marketing channels and touchpoints. The USP should be a central element of the brand's communication strategy, reinforcing the unique value proposition in every interaction.

3. Employee Training:

Ensure that employees, especially those in customer-facing roles, understand and can effectively communicate the USP. Well-trained employees can reinforce the USP during customer interactions, enhancing the overall brand experience.

4. Customer Experience:
Incorporate the USP into the customer experience to ensure it is consistently delivered. From the initial point of contact to post-purchase support, every touchpoint should reflect the unique benefits promised by the USP.

5. Brand Storytelling:
Use storytelling to communicate the USP in a compelling and relatable way. Share stories that highlight the unique benefits of the product and how it has positively impacted customers' lives.

Overcoming Common Challenges

1. Differentiation in Saturated Markets:
In highly competitive markets, differentiation can be challenging. Focus on identifying and highlighting unique benefits that truly set your product apart. Conduct thorough market research to understand unmet needs and position your product accordingly.

2. Keeping the USP Relevant:
Market conditions and consumer preferences can change over time. Continuously monitor market trends and consumer feedback to ensure the USP remains relevant. Be willing to adapt and evolve the

USP to stay aligned with current consumer needs.

3. Communicating Complex Benefits:
If the product offers complex or technical benefits, simplify the messaging to make it easily understandable. Use analogies, visuals, and customer testimonials to convey the unique value in a relatable way.

4. Maintaining Consistency:
Consistency is key to reinforcing the USP. Ensure that all marketing materials, campaigns, and customer interactions consistently communicate the USP. Regularly review and update brand guidelines to maintain consistency.

5. Balancing Creativity and Clarity:
While creativity is important, it should not overshadow the clarity of the USP. Strive for a balance between creative expression and clear communication of the unique benefits. The USP should always be easy to understand and remember.

The Unique Selling Proposition (USP) remains a powerful tool for differentiating products and driving marketing success. By analyzing successful USP campaigns, we can learn valuable lessons about the importance of emotional connection, clarity, consistency, and cultural relevance. Modern examples of strong USPs, such as those from Tesla, Amazon Prime, and Warby Parker, demonstrate the continued effectiveness of this concept in today's dynamic marketing landscape.

Adapting USPs for digital marketing involves

personalization, multi-channel consistency, engaging content, data-driven insights, and social proof. Integrating USPs into brand strategy requires alignment with brand positioning, consistent messaging, employee training, customer experience, and storytelling. Overcoming common challenges involves focusing on differentiation, keeping the USP relevant, simplifying complex benefits, maintaining consistency, and balancing creativity with clarity.

By applying these principles and strategies, businesses can create and communicate strong USPs that resonate with consumers, build brand loyalty, and achieve long-term success in the competitive marketplace.

Chapter 10:

Claude Hopkins Scientific Advertising

Claude Hopkins is often hailed as a pioneer in the advertising industry, renowned for his scientific approach to advertising. His methodologies and insights have left an indelible mark on the field, influencing generations of marketers and advertisers. His most famous work, "Scientific Advertising," remains a foundational text in understanding the principles of effective advertising.

Early Life and Career

Claude C. Hopkins was born on October 8, 1866, in Hillsdale, Michigan. Growing up in modest circumstances, Hopkins developed a strong work ethic early on. His first foray into advertising came when he was just a teenager, selling newspapers and experimenting with promotional tactics to increase sales. This early exposure to the world of commerce and marketing sparked a lifelong passion for advertising.

After completing his education, Hopkins began his career as a bookkeeper. However, his talent for writing and keen interest in marketing soon led him to pursue opportunities in advertising. His first significant role was with the Bissell Carpet Sweeper

Company, where he quickly made a name for himself by developing effective advertising campaigns that drove sales.

Key Contributions to Advertising

Claude Hopkins' career is marked by several key contributions that revolutionized the advertising industry:

1. Introduction of the Scientific Approach

Hopkins is best known for introducing a scientific approach to advertising. He believed that advertising should be based on tested and proven principles rather than guesswork or creative intuition. This approach emphasized the importance of research, testing, and measurement to optimize advertising effectiveness.

2. Emphasis on Direct Response Advertising

Hopkins was a strong advocate of direct response advertising, which focuses on generating immediate action from consumers, such as making a purchase or requesting more information. He believed that every advertisement should have a clear call to action and that its success should be measured by the tangible results it produced.

3. Use of Coupons and Sampling

One of Hopkins' significant innovations was the use of coupons and product sampling in advertising. He realized that offering consumers a low-risk way to try a product could significantly increase sales. This tactic allowed potential customers to experience the product's benefits firsthand, leading to higher conversion rates.

4. Development of Compelling Copy

Hopkins was a master copywriter who understood the power of words in influencing consumer behavior. He believed that advertising copy should be clear, concise, and focused on the consumer's needs and desires. His writing style was straightforward and persuasive, often highlighting the unique benefits and features of a product.

5. Pioneering Market Research

Hopkins emphasized the importance of understanding the target audience through market research. He conducted extensive surveys and studies to gather insights into consumer preferences, habits, and pain points. This data-driven approach allowed him to craft highly targeted and effective advertising campaigns.

Influence on the Industry

Claude Hopkins' influence on the advertising industry is profound and enduring. His scientific approach to advertising laid the groundwork for modern marketing practices and principles. Here are some of the key ways in which he shaped the industry:

1. Establishment of Advertising as a Science

Before Hopkins, advertising was often seen as an art form driven by creativity and intuition. Hopkins challenged this notion by advocating for a scientific approach that relied on data, testing, and measurable results. His work helped establish advertising as a discipline grounded in research and analysis.

2. Legacy of "Scientific Advertising"

In 1923, Hopkins published his seminal book, "Scientific Advertising," which outlined his principles and methodologies. The book became an instant classic and is still widely read and referenced by marketers today. In "Scientific Advertising," Hopkins emphasized the importance of understanding consumer psychology, testing advertising copy, and measuring the effectiveness of campaigns. His insights have become foundational concepts in the field of marketing.

3. Influence on Direct Response Marketing

Hopkins' emphasis on direct response advertising has had a lasting impact on the industry. His belief that advertising should generate immediate and measurable results continues to guide modern marketing strategies. Direct mail, infomercials, and online advertising campaigns all owe a debt to Hopkins' pioneering work in this area.

4. Pioneering Consumer-Centric Advertising

Hopkins' focus on the needs and desires of the

consumer was ahead of its time. He understood that effective advertising must resonate with the target audience by addressing their pain points and offering clear solutions. This consumer-centric approach has become a cornerstone of modern marketing, where understanding and empathizing with the customer is paramount.

5. Inspiration for Future Generations

Claude Hopkins' work has inspired countless marketers, copywriters, and advertisers. His methodologies and principles have been adopted and adapted by industry leaders, influencing the development of new advertising techniques and strategies. Prominent figures such as David Ogilvy and Rosser Reeves have cited Hopkins as a significant influence on their work.

6. Integration of Testing and Optimization

One of Hopkins' key contributions was the integration of testing and optimization into the advertising process. He believed that every element of an advertisement, from the headline to the call to action, should be tested and refined to achieve the best possible results. This approach laid the foundation for modern A/B testing and conversion rate optimization practices.

Early Career Successes and Breakthrough Campaigns

1. Bissell Carpet Sweeper Company

Hopkins' early career at the Bissell Carpet Sweeper Company provided a platform for him to hone his skills and develop his scientific approach to advertising. He created campaigns that emphasized the practical benefits of the carpet sweeper, such as ease of use and efficiency, which resonated with consumers and boosted sales.

2. Swift & Company

At Swift & Company, Hopkins applied his principles to promote various meat products. One of his notable campaigns involved distributing recipe booklets that featured Swift products, encouraging consumers to try new dishes. This approach not only increased product usage but also built brand loyalty.

3. Schlitz Beer

One of Hopkins' most famous campaigns was for Schlitz Beer. At the time, Schlitz was struggling in a competitive market. Hopkins visited the brewery to understand the production process and discovered the meticulous methods used to ensure purity and quality. He used this information to craft an advertising campaign that highlighted these unique aspects, with the slogan "The beer that made Milwaukee famous." This campaign significantly increased Schlitz's market share and demonstrated the power of highlighting unique product benefits.

4. Palmolive Soap

For Palmolive Soap, Hopkins created a campaign that emphasized the natural ingredients used in the soap, such as olive oil and palm oil. By focusing on the product's benefits for the skin, Hopkins positioned Palmolive as a premium soap that offered superior results. The campaign was highly successful and helped establish Palmolive as a leading brand in the market.

Lasting Impact and Modern Relevance

1. Integration into Modern Marketing Education

Claude Hopkins' principles are widely taught in marketing and advertising courses around the world. His emphasis on testing, research, and measurable results are fundamental concepts that continue to be relevant in the digital age. Marketing textbooks and courses often reference his work, ensuring that new generations of marketers learn from his insights.

2. Influence on Digital Marketing

Hopkins' scientific approach is particularly applicable to digital marketing, where data and analytics play a crucial role. Techniques such as A/B testing, conversion rate optimization, and data-driven decision-making are direct descendants of Hopkins' methodologies. Digital marketers continue to apply his principles to optimize online advertising campaigns, improve website performance, and enhance user experience.

3. Emphasis on ROI

Hopkins' focus on return on investment (ROI)

remains a key consideration for marketers today. In an era where marketing budgets are closely scrutinized, the ability to demonstrate the effectiveness of advertising campaigns through measurable results is more important than ever. Hopkins' legacy lives on in the emphasis on accountability and ROI in modern marketing practices.

4. Enduring Relevance of "Scientific Advertising"

"Scientific Advertising" continues to be a valuable resource for marketers. The book's timeless principles and practical advice provide a solid foundation for developing effective advertising strategies. Hopkins' emphasis on understanding consumer behavior, crafting compelling copy, and measuring results are as relevant today as they were nearly a century ago.

5. Inspiration for Creative and Analytical Balance

Hopkins' work serves as a reminder of the importance of balancing creativity with analytical rigor. While creative ideas are essential for capturing attention and engaging audiences, they must be grounded in research and tested for effectiveness. Hopkins' scientific approach encourages marketers to combine creativity with data-driven decision-making to achieve the best results.

Claude Hopkins' contributions to the advertising industry have had a lasting impact, shaping the way marketers approach their craft. His scientific approach to advertising, emphasis on direct response, use of coupons and sampling, development of compelling copy, and pioneering market research have all influenced modern marketing practices.

Hopkins' legacy is evident in the ongoing relevance of his principles, as seen in the integration of his methodologies into marketing education, the application of his ideas in digital marketing, and the enduring value of "Scientific Advertising." His work serves as both a historical foundation and a practical guide for marketers seeking to create effective, results-driven advertising campaigns.

By emphasizing the importance of understanding consumer behavior, testing and optimizing advertising elements, and focusing on measurable results, Claude Hopkins laid the groundwork for a more scientific and accountable approach to advertising. His influence continues to inspire and guide marketers in their quest to connect with consumers and drive business success.

The Principles of Scientific Advertising

Claude Hopkins, often regarded as the father of scientific advertising, revolutionized the advertising industry with his data-driven, test-and-optimize approach. His principles have laid the foundation for modern advertising strategies, emphasizing the importance of data, testing, and continuous improvement to achieve measurable results.

Data-Driven Decision-Making

1. Understanding Consumer Behavior

At the heart of data-driven decision-making is a deep understanding of consumer behavior. By analyzing data on how consumers interact with products and advertisements, marketers can gain valuable insights into what drives purchasing decisions. This involves collecting data on consumer demographics, preferences, buying patterns, and feedback.

2. Segmentation and Targeting

Data allows for precise segmentation and targeting of the audience. By dividing the market into specific segments based on characteristics such as age, gender, income, and lifestyle, advertisers can tailor their messages to resonate with each group. This ensures that the right message reaches the right audience, increasing the likelihood of a positive response.

3. Personalization

Personalization is a key aspect of data-driven advertising. By leveraging data, marketers can create personalized experiences for consumers. This can include personalized email campaigns, product recommendations, and targeted advertisements. Personalization helps to build a stronger connection with consumers, enhancing engagement and loyalty.

4. Predictive Analytics

Predictive analytics uses historical data to predict

future consumer behavior. By analyzing past trends and patterns, marketers can forecast future trends and make informed decisions. This can help in anticipating market shifts, planning marketing strategies, and optimizing advertising budgets.

5. Real-Time Analytics

Real-time analytics allows marketers to track and measure the performance of their campaigns in real-time. This provides immediate feedback on what is working and what is not, enabling quick adjustments and optimizations. Real-time data can be collected from various sources such as website analytics, social media platforms, and ad networks.

Importance of Testing and Experimentation

1. Hypothesis Testing

Testing and experimentation are fundamental principles of scientific advertising. It begins with formulating hypotheses about what might work best in an advertising campaign. For example, a hypothesis might be that a certain headline will generate more clicks than another. These hypotheses are then tested through controlled experiments.

2. A/B Testing

A/B testing, also known as split testing, is a popular method used to compare two versions of an advertisement to determine which performs better. This involves creating two variations (A and B) with a single differing element, such as the headline, image, or call to action. The versions are shown to different segments of the audience, and their performance is measured to identify the more effective version.

3. Multivariate Testing

Multivariate testing is a more complex form of testing that involves simultaneously testing multiple elements of an advertisement. This method allows marketers to understand the interactions between different elements and determine the optimal combination. While more sophisticated, multivariate testing provides deeper insights into how various factors contribute to the overall performance of the ad.

4. Control Groups

Using control groups in experiments is crucial for isolating the effects of the tested elements. A control group is a segment of the audience that does not see the experimental variations and continues to see the standard advertisement. Comparing the results from the control group with those from the test groups helps in accurately measuring the impact of the changes.

5. Continuous Improvement

Testing and experimentation should be an ongoing process. The insights gained from one round of testing should inform the next, leading to continuous improvement. This iterative approach ensures that advertising strategies are constantly refined and optimized for better performance.

Measuring and Optimizing Results

1. Key Performance Indicators (KPIs)

Measuring the effectiveness of advertising campaigns requires the identification of key performance indicators (KPIs). These are specific metrics that align with the campaign's objectives. Common KPIs include click-through rates (CTR), conversion rates, return on investment (ROI), and customer acquisition costs (CAC).

2. Data Collection Tools

Various tools are available for collecting data on advertising performance. Google Analytics, for instance, provides comprehensive insights into website traffic and user behavior. Social media platforms offer built-in analytics for tracking engagement metrics. Additionally, CRM systems can track customer interactions and sales data.

3. Analyzing Data

Data analysis involves examining the collected data to identify patterns, trends, and correlations. This can be done using statistical methods and data visualization tools. The goal is to extract actionable insights that can inform decision-making. For example, analyzing the conversion rate data might reveal that a particular ad performs better among a certain demographic.

4. Optimizing Campaigns

Optimization is the process of making adjustments to

improve campaign performance based on the insights gained from data analysis. This can involve changing ad copy, adjusting targeting parameters, reallocating budgets, or refining the call to action. Optimization should be an ongoing effort to ensure that campaigns remain effective in achieving their goals.

5. Reporting and Feedback

Regular reporting and feedback are essential for tracking progress and maintaining accountability. Reports should highlight key findings, performance metrics, and recommendations for future actions. Sharing these reports with stakeholders ensures that everyone is aligned and informed about the campaign's progress.

The Importance of Testing and Measuring Results

Testing and measuring results are critical components of scientific advertising. They provide the empirical evidence needed to validate hypotheses, understand consumer behavior, and make informed decisions. Techniques for Effective Testing

1. Randomized Controlled Trials (RCTs)

RCTs are the gold standard for testing in advertising. They involve randomly assigning participants to either the experimental group or the control group. This randomization ensures that any differences in outcomes can be attributed to the experimental variable, reducing bias and increasing the validity of the results.

2. Sequential Testing

Sequential testing is a method where tests are conducted in a sequence rather than simultaneously. This approach is useful when testing multiple variables or when resources are limited. By testing one element at a time, marketers can isolate the impact of each change and make more precise adjustments.

3. Adaptive Testing

Adaptive testing involves dynamically adjusting the test conditions based on real-time performance data. For example, if a particular ad variation is performing significantly better, more traffic can be directed to that variation. This method allows for faster optimization and can lead to quicker insights.

4. Sample Size Determination

Determining the appropriate sample size is crucial for ensuring the reliability of test results. A sample size that is too small may not provide statistically significant results, while an excessively large sample size can be resource-intensive. Statistical formulas and tools can help in calculating the optimal sample size based on the desired confidence level and margin of error.

5. Cross-Validation

Cross-validation is a technique used to assess the generalizability of test results. It involves dividing the data into multiple subsets, conducting the test on each subset, and averaging the results. This approach helps in validating that the findings are not specific to a particular subset of data and can be generalized to the broader audience.

Analyzing Data and Drawing Conclusions

1. Descriptive Statistics

Descriptive statistics provide a summary of the data, including measures such as mean, median, mode, and standard deviation. These metrics offer a snapshot of the central tendencies and variability within the data, helping to identify patterns and outliers.

2. Inferential Statistics

Inferential statistics involve making predictions or inferences about a population based on sample data. Techniques such as regression analysis, t-tests, and chi-square tests can be used to determine the statistical significance of the results and draw conclusions about the broader population.

3. Data Visualization

Data visualization tools, such as charts, graphs, and dashboards, make it easier to interpret and communicate data insights. Visual representations can highlight trends, correlations, and anomalies, making the data more accessible and actionable for decision-makers.

4. Hypothesis Testing

Hypothesis testing involves comparing the observed data to what would be expected under a null hypothesis. By calculating p-values and confidence intervals, marketers can assess whether the observed differences are statistically significant and not due to random chance.

5. Root Cause Analysis

Root cause analysis helps identify the underlying factors contributing to the observed results. This involves digging deeper into the data to uncover the reasons behind performance trends, whether positive or negative. Understanding the root causes allows for more targeted and effective optimizations.

Case Studies of Successful Testing

1. Google's AdWords Experiments

Google's AdWords platform (now Google Ads) has long been a proponent of testing and optimization. One notable case study involves a series of A/B tests conducted to improve ad copy. By testing different headlines, descriptions, and call-to-action phrases, Google identified the most effective combinations that led to higher click-through rates and conversions.

Results:

- Significant improvement in ad performance metrics.

- Enhanced understanding of what resonated with different audience segments.
- Continuous optimization based on data-driven insights.

2. Netflix's Personalized Recommendations

Netflix uses sophisticated algorithms and extensive A/B testing to optimize its personalized recommendation engine. By testing different recommendation algorithms and presentation formats, Netflix continually refines its system to provide more accurate and engaging content suggestions for users.

Results:

- Increased user engagement and retention.
- Higher satisfaction with personalized content.
- Data-driven improvements to the recommendation engine.

3. Facebook's News Feed Algorithm

Facebook constantly tests and tweaks its News Feed algorithm to improve user experience and engagement. Through a series of controlled experiments, Facebook evaluates how different content types, engagement signals, and ranking criteria impact user behavior.

Results:

- Improved relevance and quality of content in

users' News Feeds.

- Increased user engagement and time spent on the platform.

- Continuous learning and adaptation based on user feedback and data.

4. Amazon's Product Recommendations

Amazon is known for its data-driven approach to optimizing product recommendations. By conducting A/B tests on different recommendation algorithms, placement strategies, and personalization techniques, Amazon enhances its ability to suggest relevant products to customers.

Results:

- Increased sales and average order value.

- Higher customer satisfaction with personalized shopping experiences.

- Ongoing optimization based on performance data.

Applying Scientific Advertising Principles to Modern Marketing

The principles of scientific advertising, as championed by Claude Hopkins, are more relevant than ever in today's digital marketing landscape. By embracing data-driven decision-making, rigorous testing, and continuous optimization, modern marketers can achieve superior results.

Adapting USPs for Digital Marketing

1. Leveraging Big Data

The availability of big data provides unprecedented opportunities for understanding consumer behavior and preferences. Marketers can analyze vast amounts of data to identify trends, segment audiences, and personalize marketing messages at scale.

2. Advanced Analytics and AI

Advanced analytics and artificial intelligence (AI) enable more sophisticated testing and optimization. Machine learning algorithms can analyze complex data sets, predict outcomes, and recommend optimal strategies, enhancing the effectiveness of advertising campaigns.

3. Omni-Channel Integration

Digital marketing encompasses a wide range of channels, including social media, email, search engines, and mobile apps. Integrating the USP across all these channels ensures a consistent and cohesive brand message, enhancing the overall impact of marketing efforts.

4. Real-Time Adjustments

The digital environment allows for real-time adjustments to campaigns based on performance data. Marketers can quickly respond to changing conditions, optimize ad placements, and refine targeting strategies to maximize results.

Integrating USPs into Brand Strategy

1. Consistency Across Touchpoints

Ensuring that the USP is consistently communicated across all brand touchpoints strengthens brand identity and reinforces the unique value proposition. This includes everything from advertising and social media to customer service and product packaging.

2. Customer-Centric Approach

A customer-centric approach involves deeply understanding and addressing customer needs and preferences. By aligning the USP with what matters most to customers, brands can create more meaningful and impactful connections.

3. Continuous Feedback Loop

Establishing a continuous feedback loop with customers helps in refining and optimizing the USP. Regularly gathering and analyzing customer feedback provides valuable insights into how the brand is perceived and where improvements can be made.

4. Aligning with Brand Values

The USP should align with the brand's core values and mission. This alignment ensures authenticity and builds trust with customers, as the brand's promises are seen as genuine and consistent with its overall identity.

Overcoming Common Challenges

1. Navigating Data Privacy Regulations

With the increasing focus on data privacy, marketers must navigate regulations such as GDPR and CCPA. Ensuring compliance while still leveraging data for insights and personalization is a critical challenge that requires careful management.

2. Managing Data Quality

The accuracy and reliability of data are paramount for effective decision-making. Marketers must implement robust data management practices to ensure that the data used for analysis and testing is high-quality and free from biases.

3. Balancing Innovation with Proven Strategies

While innovation is important, it must be balanced with proven strategies that deliver consistent results. Marketers should adopt a test-and-learn mindset, where new ideas are rigorously tested before full implementation.

4. Keeping Pace with Technological Advancements

The rapid pace of technological advancements presents both opportunities and challenges. Marketers must stay informed about new tools and technologies, continuously updating their skills and strategies to remain competitive.

The principles of scientific advertising, as articulated by Claude Hopkins, provide a timeless framework for effective marketing. By embracing data-driven decision-making, rigorous testing, and continuous optimization, marketers can achieve measurable and impactful results. The importance of testing and measuring results cannot be overstated, as it provides the empirical evidence needed to validate hypotheses, understand consumer behavior, and make informed decisions.

Modern marketing challenges, including adapting USPs for digital marketing, integrating USPs into brand strategy, and overcoming common obstacles, can be effectively addressed by applying these principles. The case studies of successful testing from companies like Google, Netflix, Facebook, and Amazon demonstrate the power of scientific advertising in driving business success.

By continuously refining and optimizing advertising strategies based on data and insights, marketers can create more personalized, relevant, and effective campaigns that resonate with their target audiences and drive long-term growth. The legacy of Claude Hopkins lives on in the practices and methodologies that continue to shape the future of marketing and advertising.

Techniques for Writing Effective Copy

Effective advertising copy is the lifeblood of successful marketing campaigns. It captures attention, conveys value, and persuades the audience to take action. Claude Hopkins, a pioneer in scientific advertising, developed techniques that continue to influence copywriting today. This section delves into crafting persuasive copy, testing and refining it, and examining examples of effective advertising copy.

Crafting Persuasive Copy

1. Know Your Audience

Understanding your audience is the first step in crafting persuasive copy. This involves researching their needs, desires, pain points, and preferences. By knowing what drives your audience, you can tailor your message to resonate with them on a personal level.

2. Focus on Benefits, Not Features

While features describe what a product does, benefits explain how those features improve the consumer's life. Effective copy focuses on the benefits, making it clear how the product or service solves a problem or fulfills a need. For example, instead of saying, "This vacuum cleaner has a powerful motor," say, "This vacuum cleaner makes your home spotless in minutes."

3. Use Emotional Appeal

Emotional appeal is a powerful tool in persuasive copywriting. People often make purchasing decisions based on emotions, then justify them with logic. Craft copy that taps into emotions such as happiness, fear, trust, or urgency. For example, "Protect your family with our top-rated security system" appeals to the emotional need for safety and security.

4. Be Clear and Concise

Clarity and conciseness are crucial in advertising copy. Avoid jargon and complex sentences that might confuse the reader. Get straight to the point, and make sure your message is easy to understand. Short, punchy sentences often have more impact than long, convoluted ones.

5. Create a Strong Call to Action (CTA)

A compelling call to action directs the reader to take the next step, whether it's making a purchase, signing up for a newsletter, or contacting your business. Use action-oriented language that creates a sense of urgency. Phrases like "Buy Now," "Sign Up Today," or "Get Your Free Trial" are effective CTAs that prompt immediate action.

6. Build Credibility and Trust

Building credibility and trust is essential for persuading consumers. Use testimonials, reviews, case studies, and endorsements to demonstrate that others have benefited from your product or service. Highlighting guarantees and return policies can also reassure potential customers.

7. Use Storytelling

Storytelling can make your copy more engaging and memorable. By weaving a narrative that illustrates the benefits of your product or service, you can capture the reader's interest and make your message more relatable. For instance, sharing a customer's success story can vividly showcase how your product made a difference in their life.

8. Leverage Power Words

Power words are emotionally charged words that can evoke strong responses from readers. Words like "exclusive," "guaranteed," "proven," "limited-time," and "free" can make your copy more compelling. Use these words strategically to highlight key benefits and create a sense of urgency.

Testing and Refining Copy

1. A/B Testing

A/B testing, or split testing, involves comparing two versions of copy to determine which one performs better. This can be done by changing a single element, such as the headline, CTA, or body text, and measuring the response. By systematically testing different variations, you can identify the most effective copy.

2. Multivariate Testing

Multivariate testing is more complex than A/B testing as it involves testing multiple variables simultaneously. This method helps understand how different elements of your copy interact with each other. For example, you can test different combinations of headlines, images, and CTAs to see which combination yields the best results.

3. Collecting and Analyzing Data

Collect data on how your copy performs across different metrics, such as click-through rates, conversion rates, and engagement levels. Use analytics tools to track these metrics and identify patterns. Analyzing this data will provide insights into what aspects of your copy are working and what needs improvement.

4. Feedback and Iteration

Gather feedback from your audience through surveys, comments, and direct interactions. Use this feedback to refine your copy. Continuous iteration based on feedback and performance data ensures that your copy evolves and improves over time.

5. Use Heatmaps and User Behavior Tools

Heatmaps and user behavior tools can provide visual insights into how users interact with your content. These tools show where users click, scroll, and spend the most time on your page. Understanding user behavior can help you refine your copy to enhance engagement and effectiveness.

Examples of Effective Advertising Copy

1. Apple's "Think Different" Campaign

Apple's "Think Different" campaign is a classic example of effective advertising copy. The slogan was simple, memorable, and aligned with Apple's brand identity of innovation and creativity. The campaign featured influential figures like Albert Einstein and Mahatma Gandhi, positioning Apple as a brand for visionaries and non-conformists.

2. Nike's "Just Do It"

Nike's "Just Do It" is one of the most iconic slogans in advertising history. The phrase is motivational and empowering, encouraging people to take action and pursue their athletic goals. The simplicity and universality of the message have made it highly effective in resonating with a broad audience.

3. De Beers' "A Diamond is Forever"

De Beers' slogan "A Diamond is Forever" successfully positioned diamonds as a symbol of eternal love and commitment. This emotionally charged message resonated deeply with consumers and became a cultural norm, significantly boosting diamond sales.

4. Dollar Shave Club's Launch Video

Dollar Shave Club's launch video is a brilliant example of humorous and engaging copy. The video's script was witty, straightforward, and effectively communicated the value proposition: high-quality razors delivered to your door for just a few dollars a month. The video went viral, generating massive brand awareness and customer acquisition.

5. Old Spice's "The Man Your Man Could Smell Like"

Old Spice's campaign, featuring the line "The Man Your Man Could Smell Like," combined humor with a strong value proposition. The playful and memorable copy, along with a charismatic spokesperson, revitalized the brand and attracted a younger audience.

Lessons from Hopkins' Campaigns That Remain Relevant Today

Claude Hopkins' advertising principles are timeless, offering valuable lessons for modern marketers. His emphasis on data, testing, and customer-centric messaging continues to influence advertising strategies today.

Timeless Principles of Advertising

1. Scientific Approach

Hopkins championed a scientific approach to advertising, relying on data and testing to drive decisions. This principle remains fundamental in modern marketing, where data analytics and performance metrics are essential tools.

2. Direct Response Focus

Hopkins believed that advertising should prompt immediate action and be directly measurable. This focus on direct response advertising is evident in contemporary practices such as pay-per-click (PPC) advertising, email marketing, and social media campaigns.

3. Consumer-Centric Messaging

Hopkins emphasized the importance of understanding and addressing consumer needs. Crafting messages that resonate with the target audience is a core tenet of effective advertising, as relevant and personalized content drives engagement and conversions.

4. Clear and Simple Copy

Clarity and simplicity in copywriting were crucial to Hopkins. Modern advertising continues to value straightforward and easily understandable messages, as they are more likely to capture attention and drive action.

5. Testing and Optimization

Continuous testing and optimization were integral to Hopkins' methodology. A/B testing, multivariate testing, and iterative refinement are standard practices in today's marketing landscape, ensuring that campaigns are continually improved based on performance data.

Adapting Hopkins' Methods for Modern Marketing

1. Leveraging Digital Analytics

Hopkins' data-driven approach can be adapted to modern marketing by leveraging digital analytics tools. Platforms like Google Analytics, Facebook

Insights, and email marketing software provide detailed data on user behavior, campaign performance, and conversion metrics.

2. Personalization and Segmentation

Modern technology allows for advanced personalization and segmentation. Using data from various sources, marketers can create highly targeted campaigns that address specific segments of their audience, increasing relevance and effectiveness.

3. Real-Time Testing

The digital environment enables real-time testing and optimization. Marketers can quickly implement A/B tests, gather results, and make adjustments on the fly. This agility allows for more dynamic and responsive advertising strategies.

4. Multi-Channel Integration

Hopkins' principles can be applied across multiple channels, including social media, email, search engines, and display advertising. Ensuring consistency in messaging and leveraging the strengths of each channel can enhance overall campaign effectiveness.

5. Content Marketing

Hopkins' emphasis on valuable content can be extended to content marketing. By creating informative, engaging, and relevant content, brands can build trust and authority, driving long-term customer relationships.

Case Studies of Lasting Impact

1. Google AdWords

Google AdWords (now Google Ads) exemplifies the application of Hopkins' principles in a digital context. AdWords campaigns are highly data-driven, allowing for precise targeting and real-time optimization. The platform's emphasis on measurable results and direct response aligns with Hopkins' focus on accountability and performance.

2. HubSpot's Inbound Marketing

HubSpot's inbound marketing strategy leverages content to attract and engage customers, much like Hopkins' focus on valuable messaging. By providing educational content, HubSpot builds trust and authority, driving customer acquisition and retention.

3. Amazon's Recommendation Engine

Amazon's recommendation engine uses data and analytics to personalize the shopping experience. By analyzing user behavior and preferences, Amazon delivers relevant product recommendations, increasing sales and enhancing customer satisfaction. This approach embodies Hopkins' emphasis on understanding and addressing consumer needs.

4. Netflix's Personalized Content

Netflix's use of data to personalize content recommendations is another example of applying Hopkins' principles. By leveraging viewing history and preferences, Netflix creates a tailored user experience that keeps subscribers engaged and reduces churn.

5. Mailchimp's Email Marketing

Mailchimp's email marketing platform enables businesses to segment audiences, personalize messages, and conduct A/B tests. These capabilities reflect Hopkins' emphasis on targeted messaging, testing, and optimization, ensuring that email campaigns are effective and relevant.

Claude Hopkins' principles of scientific advertising have enduring relevance in today's marketing landscape. His emphasis on data-driven decision-making, consumer-centric messaging, and continuous testing and optimization provides a robust framework for creating effective advertising campaigns.

Crafting persuasive copy involves understanding the audience, focusing on benefits, using emotional appeal, and creating strong calls to action. Testing and refining copy through A/B testing, multivariate testing, and data analysis ensure continuous improvement and effectiveness.

Modern marketers can adapt Hopkins' methods by leveraging digital analytics, personalization, real-time testing, multi-channel integration, and content marketing. Case studies from companies like Google,

HubSpot, Amazon, Netflix, and Mailchimp demonstrate the lasting impact of Hopkins' principles.

By embracing these timeless principles and adapting them to modern marketing challenges, businesses can create compelling advertising that resonates with their audience, drives action, and achieves measurable results. The legacy of Claude Hopkins continues to shape the future of advertising, guiding marketers in their quest for excellence.

Chapter 11:

Jay Conrad Levinson Guerrilla Marketing

Jay Conrad Levinson is a renowned figure in the world of marketing, best known for his development of Guerrilla Marketing. This approach revolutionized how small businesses market themselves by emphasizing creativity, cost-effectiveness, and unconventional strategies. Levinson's work has had a profound impact on small business marketing, making sophisticated marketing tactics accessible to companies with limited budgets.

Early Life and Career

Jay Conrad Levinson was born on February 10, 1933, in Detroit, Michigan. From a young age, he exhibited a keen interest in the arts and storytelling, which later influenced his unique approach to marketing. Levinson attended the University of Colorado, where he earned a degree in psychology. This background in psychology would later prove instrumental in his understanding of consumer behavior and his development of marketing strategies.

Levinson began his career in the advertising industry, working for major firms such as Leo Burnett and J. Walter Thompson. During his time at these agencies, he contributed to successful campaigns for high-profile clients, including Marlboro and Kellogg's. However, Levinson became increasingly frustrated with the traditional marketing methods that relied heavily on large budgets and mainstream media.

In the 1980s, Levinson left the corporate world to focus on developing marketing strategies that could be used by small businesses. This transition marked the beginning of his groundbreaking work in Guerrilla Marketing.

Key Contributions to Marketing

Jay Conrad Levinson's contributions to marketing are significant and wide-ranging. His most notable contribution is the concept of Guerrilla Marketing, which he introduced in his seminal book "Guerrilla Marketing" published in 1984. This book and its subsequent editions have sold millions of copies worldwide and have been translated into multiple languages.

1. Introduction of Guerrilla Marketing

Guerrilla Marketing is based on the idea that small businesses can compete with larger companies by using unconventional, creative, and cost-effective marketing tactics. Levinson believed that with ingenuity and a deep understanding of the target audience, small businesses could achieve significant marketing success without a large budget.

Key principles of Guerrilla Marketing include:

- Creativity Over Budget: Emphasizing

innovative and creative approaches to marketing rather than relying on large financial investments.
- Grassroots Efforts: Leveraging grassroots and community-based marketing efforts to build brand awareness and loyalty.

- Engagement: Focusing on engaging and building relationships with customers through personalized and interactive experiences.

- Flexibility: Adapting quickly to market changes and being willing to experiment with different tactics.

- Measurability: Ensuring that marketing efforts are measurable and results-oriented, allowing businesses to track effectiveness and ROI.

2. Development of Tactical Marketing Approaches

Levinson expanded on the concept of Guerrilla Marketing by developing various tactical approaches that small businesses could implement. These tactics include:

- Viral Marketing: Creating content or campaigns designed to be shared widely and rapidly by consumers.

- Ambient Marketing: Using unconventional physical spaces for advertising, such as sidewalks, restrooms, or public transportation.

- Experiential Marketing: Creating memorable experiences for customers that leave a lasting impression.

- Buzz Marketing: Generating word-of-mouth excitement and conversation about a product or service.

- Stealth Marketing: Promoting products or services in a subtle or covert manner, often without consumers realizing they are being marketed to.

3. Emphasis on Personalization and Customer Relationships

Levinson stressed the importance of personalization and building strong customer relationships. He advocated for direct communication with customers, personalized marketing messages, and providing exceptional customer service. This customer-centric approach helps small businesses differentiate themselves and build loyalty.

4. Educational Contributions

Levinson was a prolific author, writing over 30 books on marketing and business. His works, including "Guerrilla Marketing," "Guerrilla Marketing Attack," and "Guerrilla Marketing for the New Millennium," have educated countless small business owners and marketers on effective marketing strategies. He also taught marketing at the University of California, Berkeley, and conducted workshops and seminars around the world.

Influence on Small Businesses

Jay Conrad Levinson's influence on small businesses is profound. His Guerrilla Marketing principles have empowered small businesses to compete with larger companies by leveraging creativity, innovation, and cost-effective strategies.

1. Accessibility of Marketing Knowledge

Levinson made sophisticated marketing concepts accessible to small businesses. Prior to his work, many small business owners believed that effective marketing required substantial financial resources. Levinson demonstrated that with creativity and strategic thinking, small businesses could achieve significant results without breaking the bank.

2. Leveling the Playing Field

Guerrilla Marketing leveled the playing field for small businesses, allowing them to compete with larger corporations. By focusing on unique, engaging, and unconventional tactics, small businesses could stand out in a crowded marketplace and attract attention.

3. Encouraging Innovation and Experimentation

Levinson's emphasis on creativity and experimentation encouraged small businesses to think outside the box and try new approaches. This mindset has led to innovative marketing campaigns that capture the public's imagination and drive business growth.

4. Building Strong Customer Relationships

Levinson's focus on personalization and customer relationships has helped small businesses build loyal customer bases. By prioritizing direct communication and exceptional service, small businesses can foster strong connections with their customers, leading to repeat business and positive word-of-mouth.

5. Measurable Results

Guerrilla Marketing's emphasis on measurability and results-oriented tactics has enabled small businesses to track the effectiveness of their marketing efforts. This focus on accountability ensures that marketing budgets are used efficiently and that strategies are continually refined for better performance.

Biography and Career Highlights

1. Early Career Successes

Levinson's early career in traditional advertising provided him with valuable insights into consumer behavior and marketing strategies. His work on campaigns for major brands like Marlboro and Kellogg's gave him a solid foundation in the principles of effective advertising.

2. Transition to Guerrilla Marketing

Levinson's departure from the corporate advertising world marked a pivotal moment in his career.

Frustrated with the limitations of traditional marketing methods, he set out to develop strategies that could be used by small businesses. This led to the creation of Guerrilla Marketing and the publication of his influential book.

3. Publication of "Guerrilla Marketing"

The release of "Guerrilla Marketing" in 1984 was a watershed moment in the marketing world. The book's success catapulted Levinson to prominence and established him as a thought leader in the field of small business marketing. The book's principles resonated with small business owners and marketers, leading to its widespread adoption and continued relevance.

4. Expansion of Guerrilla Marketing Principles

Levinson continued to expand on the principles of Guerrilla Marketing through his subsequent books and teachings. He explored new tactics and approaches, adapting Guerrilla Marketing to evolving market conditions and technological advancements. His work remained relevant as the marketing landscape shifted with the rise of digital and social media.

5. Educational and Speaking Engagements

In addition to his writing, Levinson was an educator and sought-after speaker. He taught marketing at the University of California, Berkeley, and conducted workshops and seminars globally. His engaging and practical presentations inspired countless entrepreneurs and marketers to adopt Guerrilla Marketing principles.

6. Legacy and Recognition

Jay Conrad Levinson's contributions to marketing have been widely recognized and celebrated. He received numerous awards and accolades throughout his career, including induction into the Direct Marketing Association Hall of Fame. His legacy continues to influence modern marketing practices and inspire small business owners to pursue innovative and cost-effective strategies.

Key Contributions to Marketing

1. Redefining Small Business Marketing

Levinson redefined small business marketing by demonstrating that effective strategies do not require large budgets. His emphasis on creativity, innovation, and engagement provided small businesses with the tools to compete with larger companies and achieve significant results.

2. Development of Cost-Effective Marketing Tactics

Levinson's development of cost-effective marketing tactics empowered small businesses to maximize their marketing budgets. By focusing on grassroots efforts, community engagement, and unconventional approaches, small businesses could achieve substantial visibility and impact.

3. Promotion of Personalized Marketing

Levinson's advocacy for personalized marketing highlighted the importance of building strong customer relationships. His emphasis on direct communication, tailored messages, and exceptional service has become a cornerstone of modern marketing practices.

4. Influence on Digital and Social Media Marketing

The principles of Guerrilla Marketing have had a lasting impact on digital and social media marketing. The emphasis on creativity, engagement, and viral potential aligns with the characteristics of successful digital campaigns. Levinson's work laid the groundwork for many of the strategies used in online marketing today.

Influence on Small Businesses

Jay Conrad Levinson's influence on small businesses extends beyond his groundbreaking work in Guerrilla Marketing. His principles have fundamentally changed how small businesses approach marketing, making sophisticated strategies accessible and effective.

1. Empowering Small Businesses

Levinson empowered small businesses by providing them with practical and actionable marketing strategies. His work gave small business owners the confidence to compete with larger companies and achieve their marketing goals.

2. Encouraging Innovation

Levinson's emphasis on creativity and experimentation encouraged small businesses to innovate and try new approaches. This mindset has led to the development of unique and memorable marketing campaigns that stand out in the marketplace.

3. Fostering Community Engagement

Levinson's focus on grassroots and community-based marketing efforts has helped small businesses build strong local connections. By engaging with their communities, small businesses can create loyal customer bases and generate positive word-of-mouth.

4. Providing Educational Resources

Levinson's books, workshops, and seminars have provided invaluable educational resources for small business owners and marketers. His practical advice and real-world examples have helped countless businesses improve their marketing efforts and achieve success.

5. Promoting Measurable Marketing

Levinson's emphasis on measurable results has instilled a culture of accountability in small business marketing. By tracking the effectiveness of their marketing efforts, small businesses can make data-driven decisions and continually refine their strategies for better performance.

Jay Conrad Levinson's contributions to the world of marketing, particularly through his development of Guerrilla Marketing, have had a profound and lasting impact on small businesses. His innovative and cost-effective strategies have empowered small businesses to compete with larger companies, foster strong customer relationships, and achieve measurable results.

Levinson's emphasis on creativity, engagement, and personalization has redefined small business marketing, making sophisticated strategies accessible to those with limited budgets. His educational resources and practical advice have inspired countless entrepreneurs and marketers to adopt Guerrilla Marketing principles and pursue innovative approaches.

The legacy of Jay Conrad Levinson continues to influence modern marketing practices, particularly in the realms of digital and social media marketing. His work remains relevant and valuable, providing small businesses with the tools to navigate the ever-evolving marketing landscape and achieve lasting success.

The Principles of Guerrilla Marketing

Jay Conrad Levinson revolutionized marketing with his introduction of Guerrilla Marketing in the 1980s. His approach empowered small businesses to compete with larger companies through creativity, ingenuity, and cost-effective strategies. Here, we explore the core principles of Guerrilla Marketing, its creative and unconventional tactics, and strategies for cost-effective marketing.

Definition and Core Principles

Definition of Guerrilla Marketing

Guerrilla Marketing refers to an unconventional marketing strategy aimed at achieving maximum exposure with minimal resources. Unlike traditional marketing, which often relies on large budgets and extensive media buys, Guerrilla Marketing emphasizes creativity, surprise, and the element of shock. It is designed to generate buzz, create memorable experiences, and engage the audience on a personal level.

Core Principles of Guerrilla Marketing

- **Creativity Over Budget**
    - Guerrilla Marketing prioritizes innovative and creative ideas over large financial investments. The focus is on out-of-the-box thinking to capture attention and engage the audience.

- **Surprise and Delight**
    - Effective Guerrilla Marketing campaigns often involve an element of surprise. By catching the audience off guard, these campaigns create memorable and impactful experiences that resonate.

- **Engagement and Interaction**
    - Engaging the audience and encouraging interaction is a key aspect of Guerrilla Marketing. This can include hands-on experiences, participatory events, and social media engagement.

- **Flexibility and Adaptability**
    - Guerrilla Marketing requires flexibility and the ability to adapt quickly to changing conditions. Marketers must be willing to experiment with different tactics and adjust their strategies based on feedback and results.

- **Local Focus and Community Engagement**
    - Many Guerrilla Marketing campaigns are locally focused, leveraging community spaces and events to reach the target audience. Building strong connections within the community can amplify the campaign's impact.

- **Cost-Effectiveness**
    - Cost-effectiveness is a cornerstone of Guerrilla Marketing. The goal is to achieve significant results without a substantial financial outlay. This

involves leveraging low-cost or free resources and maximizing the impact of every dollar spent.

- **Measurability and Results Orientation**
    - Guerrilla Marketing emphasizes measurable outcomes. Marketers should track the performance of their campaigns and use data to refine their strategies and optimize results.

Creative and Unconventional Tactics

1. Ambient Marketing

Ambient marketing involves placing advertisements in unexpected places where consumers do not anticipate seeing them. Examples include ads on public transportation, street art, or restroom mirrors. The goal is to surprise and engage the audience in their everyday environments.

Example: Coca-Cola's "Happiness Machine"

Coca-Cola installed a vending machine that dispensed free drinks and unexpected gifts (like flowers and pizzas) to people passing by. The campaign was filmed and shared online, creating a viral effect and spreading the message of happiness and generosity.

2. Viral Marketing

Viral marketing leverages the power of social media

and word-of-mouth to spread a message rapidly. The idea is to create content that is so engaging, entertaining, or informative that people feel compelled to share it with others.

Example: Old Spice's "The Man Your Man Could Smell Like"

This campaign featured humorous and memorable commercials starring Isaiah Mustafa. The ads quickly went viral, generating millions of views and significantly boosting Old Spice's sales and brand recognition.

3. Experiential Marketing

Experiential marketing creates immersive experiences that allow consumers to interact with a brand in a memorable way. This can include live events, pop-up shops, or interactive installations.

Example: Red Bull's "Stratos Jump"

Red Bull sponsored Felix Baumgartner's record-breaking skydive from the stratosphere. The event was streamed live, capturing global attention and reinforcing Red Bull's brand message of extreme energy and adventure.

4. Guerrilla Projections

Guerrilla projections involve projecting images or messages onto buildings or other public spaces. This tactic is often used to create striking visual displays that capture attention.

Example: Amnesty International's "Shadows" Campaign

Amnesty International used projections of human silhouettes on buildings to raise awareness about human rights abuses. The stark imagery and powerful message drew attention to their cause and generated significant media coverage.

5. Street Art and Graffiti

Using street art and graffiti as a marketing tactic can create visually appealing and thought-provoking campaigns. These works often blend seamlessly into the urban environment, making them more impactful.

Example: Nike's "Write the Future"

Nike commissioned street artists to create murals featuring famous athletes in urban areas around the world. The murals were visually striking and generated buzz in the lead-up to the FIFA World Cup.

6. Flash Mobs

Flash mobs involve organizing a group of people to perform a synchronized activity in a public space, surprising and entertaining bystanders. These events are often recorded and shared online.

Example: T-Mobile's "Dance"

T-Mobile organized a flash mob at Liverpool Street Station in London, where hundreds of dancers performed a choreographed routine. The event was recorded and became a viral sensation, promoting T-Mobile's message of connectivity and shared experiences.

Cost-Effective Strategies

1. Leveraging Social Media

Social media platforms offer cost-effective ways to reach a large audience. By creating engaging content and encouraging shares, likes, and comments, small businesses can amplify their message without a significant financial investment.

2. Utilizing User-Generated Content

Encouraging customers to create and share content related to a brand can be a powerful and cost-effective marketing strategy. User-generated content adds authenticity and can help build a sense of community around the brand.

3. Partnering with Influencers

Collaborating with influencers can extend a brand's reach and credibility. Influencers have established trust with their followers, and their endorsements can significantly impact brand perception and sales.

4. Hosting Events and Workshops

Hosting events and workshops can engage the local

community and provide value to potential customers. These events do not need to be expensive; they can be simple gatherings that offer useful information or fun experiences.

5. Creating Shareable Content

Creating content that is inherently shareable, such as entertaining videos, informative articles, or striking images, can help spread a brand's message organically. The key is to produce content that resonates with the target audience and encourages them to share it with their networks.

6. Leveraging Public Relations

Public relations efforts, such as press releases, media coverage, and speaking engagements, can generate buzz and visibility for a brand at a relatively low cost. Building relationships with journalists and bloggers can help secure valuable media exposure.

Creative and Cost-Effective Marketing Tactics

Examples of Guerrilla Marketing Campaigns

1. IKEA's "Moving Day"

IKEA's "Moving Day" campaign in Montreal involved placing life-sized cardboard cutouts of furniture in various public locations, such as bus stops and parks. Each cutout had a QR code that, when scanned, directed people to the IKEA website to purchase the actual item.

Lessons Learned:

- Engagement: The campaign encouraged direct interaction with the brand through QR codes.

- Visibility: The unconventional placement of the cutouts attracted attention and curiosity.

- Integration: Linking the physical cutouts to the online store provided a seamless customer journey.

2. The Blair Witch Project

The Blair Witch Project is a classic example of effective guerrilla marketing in the film industry. The filmmakers created a website with fake police reports and news articles to make it seem like the documentary was real. This created a buzz and generated significant interest in the film.

Lessons Learned:

- Mystery and Curiosity: Creating an air of mystery and curiosity can generate significant buzz and word-of-mouth.

- Viral Potential: Leveraging the internet and online forums helped spread the campaign quickly and widely.

- Low Budget, High Impact: The campaign was inexpensive but highly effective in generating interest and box office success.

3. ALS Ice Bucket Challenge

The ALS Ice Bucket Challenge involved people dumping buckets of ice water over their heads and challenging others to do the same or donate to the ALS Association. The challenge went viral on social media, raising awareness and significant funds for ALS research.

Lessons Learned:

- Engagement and Participation: Encouraging user participation can significantly amplify a campaign's reach.

- Social Media Integration: Leveraging social media platforms can help a campaign go viral and reach a global audience.

- Clear Call to Action: The challenge had a clear call to action—participate or donate—which drove results.

4. UNICEF's Dirty Water Campaign

UNICEF's Dirty Water Campaign involved placing vending machines in public places that sold "dirty water" to raise awareness about the lack of clean drinking water in many parts of the world. The vending machines offered various types of contaminated water, highlighting the different diseases they could cause.

Lessons Learned:

- Shock Value: The campaign used shock value to draw attention to a serious issue.

- Public Engagement: Placing the vending machines in high-traffic areas ensured high visibility and engagement.

- Educational Impact: The campaign effectively educated the public about the global water crisis.

Tips for Implementing Guerrilla Tactics

1. Understand Your Audience

Knowing your audience is crucial for any marketing campaign. Conduct research to understand their preferences, habits, and pain points. This will help you create campaigns that resonate and engage effectively.

2. Be Creative and Bold

Guerrilla Marketing thrives on creativity and boldness. Don't be afraid to think outside the box and take risks. The goal is to create memorable experiences that stand out and capture attention.

3. Leverage Local and Community Resources

Utilize local and community resources to amplify your campaign. This can include partnering with local businesses, participating in community events, and using public spaces for your marketing efforts.

4. Keep It Simple and Clear

While creativity is important, it's equally important to keep your message simple and clear. Ensure that your audience can quickly understand the purpose of your campaign and what action you want them to take.

5. Encourage Participation and Interaction

Encouraging participation and interaction can significantly enhance the impact of your campaign. Create opportunities for your audience to engage with your brand and share their experiences on social media.

6. Measure and Analyze Results

Tracking the performance of your Guerrilla Marketing campaigns is essential. Use analytics tools to measure engagement, reach, and ROI. Analyzing the data will provide insights into what worked and what didn't, allowing you to refine your strategies for future campaigns.

7. Be Flexible and Adaptable

Guerrilla Marketing requires flexibility and adaptability. Be prepared to make adjustments based on real-time feedback and changing conditions. This agility will help you optimize your campaigns and maximize their effectiveness.

Jay Conrad Levinson's Guerrilla Marketing principles have fundamentally changed the way small businesses approach marketing. By emphasizing creativity, engagement, and cost-effectiveness, Guerrilla Marketing enables small businesses to compete with larger companies and achieve significant results.

The core principles of Guerrilla Marketing—creativity over budget, surprise and delight, engagement and interaction, flexibility and adaptability, local focus and community engagement, cost-effectiveness, and measurability—provide a robust framework for developing impactful marketing strategies.

Through creative and unconventional tactics such as ambient marketing, viral marketing, experiential marketing, guerrilla projections, street art, and flash mobs, small businesses can capture attention and engage their audience in memorable ways. Cost-effective strategies like leveraging social media, utilizing user-generated content, partnering with influencers, hosting events, creating shareable content, and leveraging public relations further enhance the reach and impact of Guerrilla Marketing campaigns.

The success stories of campaigns like IKEA's "Moving Day," The Blair Witch Project, the ALS Ice Bucket Challenge, and UNICEF's Dirty Water Campaign illustrate the power of Guerrilla Marketing to generate buzz, drive engagement, and achieve measurable results.

By understanding their audience, being creative and bold, leveraging local resources, keeping messages simple, encouraging participation, measuring results, and staying flexible, small businesses can effectively implement Guerrilla Marketing tactics and achieve their marketing goals.

The legacy of Jay Conrad Levinson and his Guerrilla Marketing principles continue to inspire and guide marketers in their quest to create impactful, memorable, and cost-effective marketing campaigns.

Examples of Successful Guerrilla Marketing Campaigns

Guerrilla marketing campaigns have achieved remarkable success through creativity, surprise, and engagement. These campaigns often become case studies due to their innovative approaches and impactful results. Below, we explore several notable guerrilla marketing campaigns, analyze their success factors, and extract lessons for small businesses.

Case Studies of Notable Campaigns

1. Coca-Cola's "Happiness Machine"

Campaign Overview:

Coca-Cola installed vending machines in public places that dispensed not only free Cokes but also surprise items like flowers, pizzas, and sandwiches. The machine was labeled the "Happiness Machine," and the reactions of delighted consumers were filmed and shared online.

Success Factors:

- Emotional Engagement: The campaign tapped

into positive emotions by surprising people with unexpected gifts, creating joyful and memorable experiences.

- Viral Potential: The videos of happy reactions were shared widely on social media, extending the campaign's reach and impact.

- Brand Alignment: The concept of spreading happiness was perfectly aligned with Coca-Cola's brand message.

Lessons for Small Businesses:

- Create Joy: Engaging consumers with positive emotions can build a strong connection with your brand.

- Leverage Social Media: Sharing engaging content on social media can amplify your campaign's reach.

- Align with Brand Values: Ensure your guerrilla marketing tactics reflect your brand's core values and messaging.

2. ALS Ice Bucket Challenge

Campaign Overview:

The ALS Ice Bucket Challenge encouraged people to dump a bucket of ice water over their heads, record it, and challenge others to do the same or donate to ALS research. The challenge went viral, with numerous celebrities and public figures participating.

Success Factors:

- Engagement: The challenge was participatory, making people feel involved and part of a larger movement.

- Social Proof: High-profile endorsements and widespread participation helped legitimize and spread the campaign.

- Clear Call to Action: The campaign had a straightforward and compelling call to action—participate or donate.

Lessons for Small Businesses:

- Encourage Participation: Campaigns that involve consumer participation can significantly boost engagement and reach.

- Utilize Influencers: Collaborate with influencers to gain credibility and extend your campaign's reach.

- Provide a Clear CTA: Ensure your campaign includes a clear and compelling call to action.

3. The Blair Witch Project

Campaign Overview:

Before the release of the horror film "The Blair Witch

Project," the filmmakers created a website featuring fake news reports, police reports, and interviews that made it appear as if the documentary was real. This generated significant buzz and curiosity about the film.

Success Factors:

- Mystery and Curiosity: The campaign's mysterious nature piqued people's curiosity and generated word-of-mouth buzz.

- Viral Marketing: The intriguing and ambiguous content encouraged people to share and discuss it online.

- Low Budget: The campaign was inexpensive but highly effective in creating anticipation and hype.

Lessons for Small Businesses:

- Generate Curiosity: Creating a sense of mystery can intrigue your audience and stimulate word-of-mouth marketing.

- Leverage the Internet: Use websites and social media to create engaging and shareable content.

- Maximize Budget: Innovative and creative strategies can yield significant results even with limited budgets.

4. UNICEF's "Dirty Water" Campaign

Campaign Overview:

UNICEF placed vending machines in high-traffic areas that sold different types of "dirty water" to raise awareness about the lack of clean drinking water in many parts of the world. Each button on the machine corresponded to a specific waterborne disease, such as cholera or dysentery.

Success Factors:

- Shock Value: The campaign's shocking and thought-provoking approach drew significant attention.

- Educational Impact: It effectively educated the public about global water issues in a tangible way.

- Public Engagement: The placement of the vending machines in public areas ensured high visibility and engagement.

Lessons for Small Businesses:

- Create Impact: Use shocking or provocative elements to draw attention to important issues.

- Educate Consumers: Incorporate educational components to inform and engage your audience.

- Utilize High-Traffic Areas: Place your campaigns in locations with high foot traffic to maximize visibility.

Analysis of Success Factors
1. Creativity and Innovation

All successful guerrilla marketing campaigns share a common trait: creativity. These campaigns stand out because they break the mold and offer something unexpected and original. Innovation captures attention and generates buzz.

2. Emotional Engagement

Emotional engagement is crucial for making campaigns memorable. Whether it's joy, surprise, curiosity, or shock, eliciting an emotional response ensures that the audience remembers the campaign and shares it with others.

3. Social Media Amplification

The role of social media in amplifying guerrilla marketing campaigns cannot be overstated. By creating shareable content, campaigns can achieve viral status, reaching a far larger audience than initially targeted.

4. Alignment with Brand Values

Effective campaigns align closely with the brand's core values and messaging. This ensures authenticity and helps build a coherent brand image that resonates with the target audience.

5. Cost-Effectiveness

Guerrilla marketing thrives on cost-effective strategies. These campaigns often achieve significant impact without substantial financial investment, demonstrating that creativity can outweigh budget constraints.

6. Clear Call to Action

A clear and compelling call to action guides the audience towards the desired outcome, whether it's making a donation, visiting a website, or purchasing a product. This clarity ensures that the campaign drives tangible results.

Lessons for Small Businesses

1. Embrace Creativity

Small businesses should prioritize creativity in their marketing efforts. Think outside the box and develop unique approaches that differentiate your brand from competitors.

2. Focus on Emotional Connections

Build campaigns that connect with your audience on an emotional level. Whether through humor, surprise, or empathy, emotional engagement can significantly enhance the impact of your marketing efforts.

3. Utilize Social Media

Leverage social media platforms to share your campaigns and engage with your audience. Encourage sharing and participation to amplify your reach.

4. Align with Your Brand

Ensure that your guerrilla marketing tactics are consistent with your brand's values and messaging. Authenticity is key to building trust and credibility with your audience.

5. Optimize Your Budget

Use cost-effective strategies to maximize your marketing budget. Guerrilla marketing proves that you don't need a large budget to achieve significant results—creativity and innovation can make a substantial impact.

6. Provide Clear Directions

Include a clear call to action in your campaigns. Guide your audience towards the desired outcome, making it easy for them to engage with your brand.

Adapting Guerrilla Marketing Strategies for the Digital Age

The digital age presents new opportunities and challenges for guerrilla marketing. Integrating traditional guerrilla tactics with digital marketing, leveraging social media and online platforms, and staying ahead of future trends are essential for success.

Integrating Guerrilla Tactics with Digital Marketing

1. Hybrid Campaigns

Combining physical and digital elements can enhance the impact of guerrilla marketing campaigns. For example, a street art installation could include a QR code that directs viewers to a related online experience or social media campaign.

Example: KitKat's "Break Bench"

KitKat placed benches in public spaces with the slogan "Have a Break, Have a KitKat." The benches included QR codes that led to online content, encouraging people to share their "break" experiences on social media.

2. Interactive Digital Experiences

Creating interactive digital experiences can engage consumers and enhance their connection with your brand. This can include online games, virtual reality experiences, or interactive videos.

Example: IKEA's "Place" App

IKEA's augmented reality app allows users to visualize how furniture will look in their homes. This interactive experience enhances engagement and helps customers make informed purchasing decisions.

3. User-Generated Content Campaigns

Encouraging user-generated content (UGC) can amplify your campaign's reach and authenticity. Create challenges or contests that prompt users to share their experiences or creations related to your brand.

Example: GoPro's UGC Campaign

GoPro encourages users to share their action-packed videos using the hashtag #GoPro. This UGC strategy not only provides authentic content but also showcases the versatility of GoPro cameras.

4. Real-Time Marketing

Real-time marketing leverages current events or trends to create timely and relevant content. This approach can generate buzz and engage audiences who are already interested in the topic.

Example: Oreo's "Dunk in the Dark"

During the 2013 Super Bowl blackout, Oreo quickly tweeted "You can still dunk in the dark." This timely and clever response went viral, showcasing the power of real-time marketing.

Leveraging Social Media and Online Platforms

1. Viral Challenges and Hashtags

Creating viral challenges and branded hashtags can boost engagement and reach on social media platforms. Encourage users to participate and share their experiences using the designated hashtag.

Example: #ShareACoke

Coca-Cola's #ShareACoke campaign invited people to find bottles with their names and share photos on social media. The personalized approach and viral hashtag significantly boosted engagement and sales.

2. Influencer Collaborations

Partnering with influencers can extend your reach and credibility. Influencers have established relationships with their followers, making their endorsements powerful and impactful.

Example: Daniel Wellington's Influencer Strategy

Daniel Wellington, a watch brand, collaborated with influencers to promote its products. The influencers shared stylish photos wearing the watches, driving brand awareness and sales.

3. Interactive Social Media Content

Interactive content, such as polls, quizzes, and live videos, can enhance engagement on social media platforms. Encourage your audience to participate and interact with your brand in real-time.

Example: BuzzFeed Quizzes

BuzzFeed's engaging quizzes are widely shared on social media, driving traffic to their website and increasing brand visibility.

4. Storytelling Through Video

Video content is highly engaging and shareable. Use storytelling techniques to create compelling videos that capture your audience's attention and convey your brand message effectively.

Example: Always' "Like a Girl" Campaign

Always' "Like a Girl" video challenged gender stereotypes and encouraged viewers to rethink the phrase "like a girl." The powerful storytelling resonated with audiences and went viral.

Future Trends in Guerrilla Marketing

1. Augmented Reality (AR) and Virtual Reality (VR)

AR and VR technologies offer new possibilities for immersive and interactive marketing experiences. Brands can create virtual environments or enhance real-world experiences with digital elements.

Example: Pokémon GO

The Pokémon GO app uses AR to create an interactive gaming experience in the real world. The game's success demonstrates the potential of AR in engaging and captivating audiences.

2. Personalization and AI

Artificial intelligence (AI) enables highly personalized marketing experiences. AI can analyze consumer data to deliver tailored content and recommendations, enhancing engagement and conversion rates.

Example: Netflix's Recommendation Engine

Netflix uses AI to personalize content recommendations based on user behavior. This personalized approach keeps subscribers engaged and satisfied.

3. Sustainability and Social Responsibility

Consumers increasingly value sustainability and social responsibility. Brands that incorporate these values into their marketing strategies can build stronger connections with their audience.

Example: Patagonia's Environmental Campaigns

Patagonia's marketing campaigns emphasize environmental conservation and sustainability. Their commitment to these values resonates with eco-conscious consumers and strengthens brand loyalty.

4. Integration with IoT (Internet of Things)

The Internet of Things (IoT) connects everyday objects to the internet, enabling new marketing opportunities. Brands can use IoT devices to deliver personalized and contextually relevant content.

Example: Smart Home Assistants

Smart home assistants like Amazon's Alexa can provide personalized product recommendations and integrate with other IoT devices to enhance the user experience.

Guerrilla marketing continues to evolve, offering creative and cost-effective strategies for small businesses to compete with larger companies. By analyzing successful guerrilla marketing campaigns, small businesses can learn valuable lessons and adapt these strategies to their own needs.

The integration of guerrilla tactics with digital marketing, leveraging social media and online platforms, and staying ahead of future trends are crucial for maximizing the impact of guerrilla marketing efforts. Hybrid campaigns, interactive digital experiences, user-generated content, and real-time marketing are effective ways to combine traditional guerrilla tactics with digital strategies.

Future trends such as augmented reality, virtual reality, personalization through AI, sustainability, and IoT integration will shape the landscape of guerrilla marketing. By embracing these trends and continuing to innovate, small businesses can create impactful, memorable, and cost-effective marketing campaigns that resonate with their audience and drive success.

The legacy of Jay Conrad Levinson's Guerrilla

Marketing principles remains strong, inspiring marketers to think creatively, engage emotionally, and achieve significant results with limited resources. By applying these principles and adapting to the digital age, small businesses can thrive in an ever-evolving marketing landscape.

Chapter 12:

Shaping the Future Integrating Lessons from the Masters

The marketing world has been shaped by numerous pioneers whose insights and principles continue to influence modern practices. Integrating lessons from these masters into today's marketing strategies can help businesses navigate the ever-evolving landscape and stay ahead of the competition.

Recap of Key Lessons from Each Marketing Master

Claude Hopkins - Scientific Advertising

Key Insights and Principles:

- Data-Driven Decision Making: Hopkins emphasized the importance of basing marketing decisions on data and research rather than intuition.

- Testing and Experimentation: Continuous testing and refinement of marketing strategies to optimize results.

- Clear and Direct Messaging: Crafting straightforward and persuasive advertising copy that focuses on the consumer's needs and desires.

Major Themes:

- The scientific approach to advertising.
- The importance of measurable results and accountability.
- Consumer-centric advertising that speaks directly to the target audience.

Rosser Reeves - Unique Selling Proposition (USP)

Key Insights and Principles:

- Unique Selling Proposition: The idea that every product must have a unique benefit that distinguishes it from competitors.
- Clear and Consistent Messaging: Maintaining a clear and consistent message across all marketing channels.
- Focus on Benefits: Highlighting the specific benefits that the product offers to the consumer.

Major Themes:

- Differentiation through unique benefits.
- Consistency in advertising messages.

- The power of a strong USP in driving consumer choice.

Jay Conrad Levinson - Guerrilla Marketing

Key Insights and Principles:

- Creativity Over Budget: Emphasizing creativity and innovation over large marketing budgets.

- Engagement and Interaction: Creating campaigns that engage and interact with the audience.

- Cost-Effective Strategies: Using low-cost or no-cost marketing tactics to achieve significant impact.

Major Themes:

- The power of creativity and innovation in marketing.

- The importance of engagement and interaction with the audience.

- Achieving significant results with cost-effective strategies.

David Ogilvy - The Father of Advertising

Key Insights and Principles:

- Research and Understanding: The importance of thorough research and understanding the

consumer.
- Brand Image: Building and maintaining a strong brand image.

- Long-Term Focus: Focusing on long-term brand building rather than short-term sales.

Major Themes:

The significance of research and consumer insights. Building and sustaining a strong brand image. Long-term focus in marketing strategy.

Strategies for Integrating These Lessons into Modern Marketing Practices

1. Implementing Data-Driven Decision Making

Practical Tips:

- Use Analytics Tools: Utilize tools like Google Analytics, social media analytics, and CRM systems to gather and analyze data.

- A/B Testing: Regularly conduct A/B tests to compare different versions of marketing materials and determine which performs better.

- Customer Surveys and Feedback: Collect feedback from customers to understand their needs and preferences better.

Real-World Example:

E-commerce Platforms: Online retailers use data analytics to track user behavior, optimize website layouts, and personalize product recommendations.

2. Crafting a Strong Unique Selling Proposition (USP)

Practical Tips:

- Identify Unique Benefits: Conduct competitor analysis to identify unique features or benefits of your product.

- Clear Messaging: Ensure that your USP is clearly communicated in all marketing materials.

- Consistent Branding: Maintain consistency in how the USP is presented across different channels.

Real-World Example:

Apple: Apple's USP of sleek design and user-friendly technology is consistently communicated across all their marketing channels.

3. Leveraging Guerrilla Marketing Tactics

Practical Tips:

- Think Outside the Box: Develop creative and unconventional marketing ideas that can capture attention.

- Engage the Community: Use local events, public spaces, and community engagement to spread your message.

- Viral Potential: Create content that has the potential to go viral on social media.

Real-World Example:

Taco Bell: Taco Bell's "#OnlyInTheApp" campaign used guerrilla marketing tactics to drive app downloads by offering exclusive deals and engaging content.

4. Building a Strong Brand Image

Practical Tips:

- Consistent Branding: Ensure all marketing materials reflect a consistent brand image and voice.

- High-Quality Content: Produce high-quality content that aligns with your brand values and resonates with your target audience.

- Brand Storytelling: Use storytelling to convey your brand's history, mission, and values.

Real-World Example:

Nike: Nike's branding consistently emphasizes inspiration, athleticism, and innovation through its

"Just Do It" campaign and athlete endorsements.

The Importance of Continuous Learning and Adaptation

Staying Updated with Industry Trends

Practical Tips:

- Regular Training: Invest in continuous learning and professional development through courses, webinars, and workshops.

- Industry Publications: Subscribe to industry publications, blogs, and newsletters to stay informed about the latest trends and innovations.

- Networking: Attend industry conferences and networking events to exchange ideas and learn from peers.

Real-World Example:

Digital Marketers: Digital marketing professionals regularly update their skills in SEO, social media marketing, and content marketing to keep pace with changing algorithms and platforms.

Adapting to Changes in the Marketing Landscape

Practical Tips:

- Agile Marketing: Implement agile marketing

practices that allow for quick adjustments based on market feedback.

- Consumer Insights: Continuously gather and analyze consumer insights to adapt your strategies to changing preferences.

- Technology Adoption: Embrace new technologies that enhance marketing efficiency and effectiveness.

Real-World Example:

Retailers During COVID-19: Many retailers quickly adapted to the pandemic by enhancing their e-commerce capabilities, offering curbside pickup, and using digital marketing to reach home-bound consumers.

Emerging Trends and the Future of Marketing

Predictions for the Future of Marketing

1. Personalization at Scale

- Advanced AI and Machine Learning: AI and machine learning will enable more personalized marketing at scale, delivering tailored content and recommendations based on individual user data.

- Hyper-Targeted Campaigns: Marketers will be able to create hyper-targeted campaigns that address the specific needs and preferences of small audience segments.

2. Increased Focus on Privacy and Ethics

- Data Privacy Regulations: Growing concerns over data privacy will lead to stricter regulations and a greater emphasis on ethical data collection and usage.

- Transparent Practices: Brands will need to adopt transparent data practices to build trust with consumers.

New Technologies and Innovations

1. Augmented Reality (AR) and Virtual Reality (VR)

- Immersive Experiences: AR and VR will provide more immersive and interactive marketing experiences, allowing consumers to engage with products in new ways.

- Virtual Try-Ons: Retailers will use AR to offer virtual try-ons for clothing, accessories, and even makeup.

2. Voice Search and Voice Commerce

- Voice-Activated Assistants: The rise of voice-activated assistants like Amazon's Alexa and Google Home will change how consumers search for information and make purchases.

- Optimizing for Voice Search: Marketers will need to optimize their content for voice search to ensure visibility and accessibility.

3. Blockchain Technology

- Transparent Transactions: Blockchain can enhance transparency and security in digital advertising, reducing fraud and building trust.

- Smart Contracts: Smart contracts can automate and verify advertising transactions, ensuring fair and accurate compensation for all parties involved.

4. AI-Driven Content Creation

- Automated Content: AI tools will assist in creating high-quality content quickly, from blog posts to social media updates.

- Predictive Analytics: AI-driven predictive analytics will help marketers anticipate consumer behavior and trends, allowing for more proactive and effective strategies.

Integrating lessons from marketing masters like Claude Hopkins, Rosser Reeves, Jay Conrad Levinson, and David Ogilvy provides a robust foundation for developing effective modern marketing strategies. Their principles of data-driven decision-making, unique selling propositions, creativity, and strong brand building remain relevant and essential.

Implementing these lessons involves leveraging modern tools and technologies, embracing creativity, and maintaining a consumer-centric approach. Continuous learning and adaptation are crucial in the fast-paced marketing landscape, ensuring that businesses stay ahead of trends and effectively meet consumer needs.

Emerging trends and technologies such as AI, AR, VR, blockchain, and voice search are set to shape the future of marketing. By staying informed and adaptable, marketers can harness these innovations to create impactful and engaging campaigns that drive business success.

The future of marketing will be characterized by personalization, transparency, and technological integration. By integrating the timeless principles of marketing masters with modern practices and emerging trends, businesses can build strong, lasting connections with their audiences and achieve sustainable growth.